D1367301

A New Owner's
Guide to
POMERANIANS

JG-145

Overleaf: Pomeranian photographed by John Ashbey

Opposite Page: Pomeranian photographed by Robert Smith

The Publisher wishes to acknowledge the owners of the dogs in this book: Diana Castro, Annette Davis, Dolores Eitelberg, Christine Jaffe, Pat Jaro, Shirley Leu, Susan Lucatorto, Janet Lucido, Eileen Maser, Julie Moreno, Susann Philbrook, Gale Sharland, Dr. Jeffrey Strom, DVM, Donna Lynn Wright.

Photographers: John Ashbey, Paulette Braun, Tara Darling, Isabelle Francais, Gilbert Photo, Mike Johnson, Kohler Photo, Celia Ooi, Linda Rowe, Vince Serbin, Robert Smith, Missy Yuhl.

The author acknowledges the contribution of Judy Iby to the following chapters: Health Care, Sport of Purebred Dogs, Identification and Finding the Lost Dog, Traveling with Your Dog, and Behavior and Canine Communication.

The portrayal of canine pet products in this book is for general instructive value only; the appearance of such products does not necessarily constitute an endorsement by the authors, the publisher, or the owners of the dogs portrayed in this book.

© **Copyright T.F.H. Publications, Inc.**

Distributed in the UNITED STATES to the Pet Trade by T.F.H. Publications, Inc., 1 TFH Plaza, Neptune City, NJ 07753; on the Internet at www.tfh.com; in CANADA by Rolf C. Hagen Inc., 3225 Sartelon St., Montreal, Quebec H4R 1E8; Pet Trade by H & L Supplies Inc., 27 Kingston Crescent, Kitchener, Ontario N2B 2T6; in ENGLAND by T.F.H. Publications, PO Box 74, Havant PO9 5TT; in AUSTRALIA AND THE SOUTH PACIFIC by T.F.H. (Australia), Pty. Ltd., Box 149, Brookvale 2100 N.S.W., Australia; in NEW ZEALAND by Brooklands Aquarium Ltd., 5 McGiven Drive, New Plymouth, RD1 New Zealand; in SOUTH AFRICA by Rolf C. Hagen S.A. (PTY.) LTD., P.O. Box 201199, Durban North 4016, South Africa; in JAPAN by T.F.H. Publications. Published by T.F.H. Publications, Inc.

MANUFACTURED IN THE
UNITED STATES OF AMERICA
BY T.F.H. PUBLICATIONS, INC.

A NEW OWNER'S GUIDE TO
POMERANIANS

JULIE MORENO

Contents

1999 Edition

The energetic and playful Pomeranian
makes a great playmate for gentle
children.

The adaptable and good-natured
Pomeranian is always ready to have
some fun with his owners.

The Pomeranian has a long history as a companion to man.

The Pomeranian has an engaging personality and an alert, intelligent expression.

The Pomeranian possesses an abundant double coat that requires regular grooming.

HISTORY of the Pomeranian

The history of the Pomeranian can be traced back to antiquity, albeit by other names at other times. It seems a well-established fact that, aided by various steps and crosses, most breeds of dog have descended from *Canis lupus*, the wolf, particularly from the northern branch of the family known as the Northern European Gray Wolf.

How long it took for the wolf to move out of the forest and into man's cave dwellings is a point of conjecture. However, it seems obvious that early man's observation of the wolf could easily have taught him some effective hunting techniques that he, too, would be able to use advantageously. Also, many of the wolf's social habits might have seemed strikingly familiar to early man. The association grew from there.

Although it may seem unlikely from looking at the Pomeranian, all of today's domesticated dogs have descended from the wolf.

Wolves that could assist in satisfying the unending human need for food were, of course, most highly prized. As the man-wolf relationship developed throughout the ages, it also became obvious that certain descendants of these increasingly domesticated wolves could be used by man to assist in survival pursuits in addition to hunting. Also highly valued were those wolves that were large enough to assist in hauling, or the *wolf-cum-dog* that made some kind of warning sound when a marauding neighbor or beast of prey threatened.

Throughout the centuries, many descendants of the original wolf stock would acquire great anatomical changes with man's intervention and breeding manipulation. However, long before man began to manipulate the size and shape of *Canis familiaris* (the domestic dog), there existed a branch of the family *canid* that, because of its close proximity to wolf ancestry, retained many of the wolf's physical characteristics.

Like their undomesticated ancestors, these dogs maintained characteristics that protected them from the rugged environment of northern Europe. Weather-resistant coats

protected them from rain and cold. A long coarse outer coat shed snow and rain, and a dense undercoat insulated against sub-zero temperatures. These coats were especially abundant around the neck and chest, thereby offering double protection to the vital organs.

Plumed tails could cover and protect the nose and mouth if the animal was forced to sleep in the snow. Small prick ears were not easily frostbitten or frozen. The muzzle had sufficient length to warm the frigid air before it reached the lungs. Leg length was sufficient to keep the chest and abdomen above the snow line. Tails were carried horizontally or up over the back, rather than trailing behind in the snow.

The spitz-type dogs, which are the ancestors of the Pomeranian, had weather-resistant double coats and plumed tails to protect the nose and mouth from snow.

Skeletal remains of these early wolf descendants have been found throughout northern and central Europe, northern Asia, and the Arctic regions of North America. They stand as the forerunners of what are commonly referred to as the Arctic or Nordic breeds.

This group can be divided into four categories: hunting dogs (Norwegian Elkhound, Chow Chow, and Karelian Bear Dog), draft dogs (Alaskan Malamute, Siberian Husky), herding dogs (Samoyed, Swedish, and Finnish Lapphunds), and companion dogs (including most of the Spitz-type dogs—German Spitz, Japanese Spitz, Pomeranian, and Volpino Italiano).

One specific branch of this family was known as *Canis familiaris palustris,* or more commonly and interchangeably known as both "the dog of the lake" and "peat bog dog." Skeletons of these Spitz-type dogs have been found in many

Once used as a protection dog that would sound the alarm against danger, the Pomeranian remains a faithful and devoted companion to man.

places throughout northern Europe and are said to have existed in the late Stone Age. The exact role of the dogs in the lives of the tribes they lived with cannot be fully identified. Some canine historians suggest that these Spitz dogs may well have served as what we now have come to think of as guard dogs—sounding the alarm by barking when danger threatened. The alert nature, rapid vocal response, and protective devotion to home and hearth of today's Spitz breeds certainly give credibility to this belief.

The adorable Pomeranian has appeared in commercials and advertisement for decades. This poster depicts two attractive redheads.

THE SPITZ BREEDS IN GERMANY

The Spitz breeds had already become popular in Germany by the early 1500s. Count Eberhard zu Sayne, a baron who resided in Germany's Rhine Valley, is the first to have been known to refer to the dogs as "Spitz." The word Spitz is German for "sharp point." The count described the dogs as having no real interest in hunting, but total dedication to master and to protecting home and property. Evidently, the Count had such a great influence in Germany that, from his first usage of the term "Spitz" in 1540, the word was not only included in the German vocabulary, but also in dictionaries from that point on.

The dogs came in many sizes and colors, each being identified by a separate name. They all, however, shared the same physical characteristics that had distinguished them for many centuries prior. Historically, dog breeds and varieties within breeds have been developed in the various towns and villages of Europe and Great Britain quite simply as a result of the color and size preferences of influential individuals or by common interest of the residents. The varieties in different areas often took on the name of the town or village in which they were developed. At other times, names referred to the particular duties assigned to the dogs.

The Spitz dogs became popular in Germany, where they were divided into varieties by size.

For our purposes, it is probably more useful to divide the German Spitz varieties by size. This classification was originally used in Germany and is used today by the Federacion Cynologique Internationale (FCI), which is the canine governing authority throughout Europe.

The Wolfspitz is the largest of the five German Spitz breeds. He stands approximately 18 in. or more at the shoulder. The only color allowed is gray. It is believed the Keeshond descended from this variety.

The next largest is the Gross Spitz, sometimes called the Giant Spitz, which stands 16 in. and above at the shoulder. Colors are black, brown, and orange.

The Mittelspitze or Standard Spitz is, ideally, 11 to 14 in. He can be black, brown, wolf gray, and orange.

The Kleinspitz or Small Spitz is bred in black, brown, wolf gray, and orange and measures 8 $^1/_2$ to 11 in. The smallest of the German Spitz is the Zwergspitz or Dwarf Spitz. This variety can be black, brown, wolf gray, and orange and measures less than 8 $^1/_2$ in.

While size and color separated the varieties in Germany, it should be remembered that, as they do now, the varieties continued to retain their basic look. The Spitz enjoyed great popularity both in Germany and abroad. By the 1700s, this popular dog of British society was called, simply, the Spitz. The dogs were a particular favorite of Queen Charlotte of England, who was born in Germany and remembered the dogs from her childhood homeland.

Charlotte had obtained her dogs from the area around Pomerania, which was particularly noted for the exceptional quality of its dogs at the time. These Spitz were later called "Pomeranians" by the Queen, although no breed has ever been known by this name in Germany.

By the 1800s, the Pomeranians (originally Spitz) gained tremendous popularity, even among England's commoners. The dogs weighed about 20 to 30 pounds and were said to be about 18 in. at the shoulder. It was not until 1870, however, that the Pomeranian was officially recognized by The Kennel Club in England. The first show at which the breed was eligible to compete was held in June 1871.

The ascent of Queen Victoria to the British throne was to forever change the character of what was referred to as the Pomeranian. While traveling throughout Italy, Victoria, an avid dog fancier, found a red sable Spitz that weighed only 12 pounds and returned to Great Britain with him. Named Windsor's Marco, he became her constant companion. Victoria entered little Marco as a Pomeranian at a show in London just two months after a specialty club for the Pomeranian had been organized. Marco won at the show and created a minor sensation, launching a demand for "Pomeranians" of his size and color.

For a time, both the larger and smaller sable-colored dogs were shown simultaneously. Eventually, the smaller dogs gained such a foothold that the larger dogs that had formerly carried the name Pomeranian fell from favor. From that point on, the diminutive variety retained the name Pomeranian.

The mixed size and type heritage of the breed continued to plague Pomeranian breeders and fanciers for many generations, but, as only the English can, they persevered. By the time the breed sparked interest in America, it was beginning to show some signs of stabilizing itself with regard to the desired "look."

THE POMERANIAN IN AMERICA

The Pomeranian was granted full breed recognition by the American Kennel Club (AKC) in 1900, and it was at that time that the American Pomeranian Club was organized. Recognition of the group as an official member of the AKC came in 1909.

Erratic size continued to plague American breeders as well. However, there was no doubt that the tiniest of the dogs gained favor rapidly, not only among dyed-in-the-wool breeder-exhibitors, but by the public as well. It was not long before American breeders, with the help of English imports and their own ingenuity, developed a Pomeranian that not only consistently bred true, but was so attractive he became one of the country's favorite small dogs.

Throughout the years, devoted US Pomeranian breeders developed a dog that was consistently bred true and attractive enough to become a favorite of many.

Interest in the breed was maintained throughout both World Wars and continues to enjoy great popularity to this day. The Pomeranian has ranked among the top ten breeds registered by the AKC since 1994.

CHARACTERISTICS of the Pomeranian

Before anyone tries to decide whether or not the Pomeranian is the correct breed for him, a larger, more important question must be asked. That question is, "Should I own a dog at all?" Dog ownership is a serious and time-consuming responsibility that should not be entered into lightly. Failure to understand this can make what should be a rewarding relationship one of sheer drudgery. It is also one of the primary reasons that thousands of unwanted dogs end their lives in humane or resuce societies and animal shelters throughout America.

The Pomeranian has a number of unique qualities that make him an adaptable and amiable breed.

If the prospective dog owner lives alone and conditions are conducive to dog ownership, all he or she needs to do is be sure that there is a strong desire to make the necessary commitment that dog

An adorable Pom puppy may be irresistible, but make sure that the decision to bring one into your home has been carefully considered.

ownership entails. In the case of family households, the situation is a much more complicated one. It is vital that the person who will actually be responsible for the dog's care really wants a dog.

In many households, mothers are most often given the additional responsibility of caring for the family pets. Children are away at school all day. Father is at work. Often, it is the mother, even the mother who works outside the home, who is saddled with the additional chores of housebreaking, feeding, and trips to the veterinary hospital. What was supposed to be a family affair eventually becomes another responsibility for Mom.

Nearly all children love puppies and dogs and will promise anything to get one. But childhood enthusiasm can wane very quickly, and it will be up to the adults in the family to ensure that the dog receives proper care. Children should be taught responsibility, but to expect a living, breathing, and needy animal to teach a child this lesson is incredibly indifferent to the needs of the animal.

There are also many households in which the entire family is gone from early morning until late in the day. The question that must be asked then is, "Who will provide food for the dog

and access to the outdoors if the dog is expected not to relieve himself in the house?" This is something that can probably be worked out with an adult dog, but it is totally unfair to expect a young puppy to be left alone the entire day.

If an individual or family finds that they are capable of providing the proper home for a dog or puppy, suitability of breed must also be considered. In this case, it might be worthwhile to look at the difference between owning a purebred dog and one of mixed ancestry.

THE CASE FOR THE PUREBRED DOG

A mixed breed can give you as much love and devotion as a purebred dog. However, the manner in which the dog does this and how his personality, energy level, and the amount of care he requires will suit an individual's lifestyle are major considerations. With a purebred dog, most of these considerations are predictable to a marked degree, even if the dog is purchased as a very young puppy. A puppy of uncertain parentage will not give you this assurance.

All puppies are cute and fairly manageable, but someone who lives in a two-room apartment will find life difficult with a dog that grows to the size of a Great Dane. Nor is the mountain climber or marathon runner going to be happy with a short-nosed breed that has difficulty catching its breath simply walking across the street on a hot summer day.

An owner who expects his or her dog to sit quietly by their side while his master watches television or reads is not going to be particularly happy with a high-strung, off-the-wall dog whose rest requirements are only 30 seconds out of every 10 hours! Likewise, the outdoorsman is not going to be particularly happy with a long-coated breed that attracts every burr, leaf, and insect in all of nature.

The Pomeranian's loving and friendly disposition makes him a welcomed addition to most families.

Knowing the kind of dog that best suits your lifestyle is not just a consideration—it is paramount to the foundation of your lifelong relationship with the dog. If the dog you are considering does not fit your lifestyle, the relationship simply will not last.

In terms of grooming, the Pomeranian is a high-maintenance dog. The time you want to spend on grooming must be a consideration before choosing a breed.

LIFE WITH A POMERANIAN

All of the foregoing applies to whether or not you should own a Pomeranian. Furthermore, as appealing as an adorable Pom puppy might be, remember he is a long-coated dog that requires care. Regular and thorough brushing is a must. When the Pom is outdoors, he is no less a dog than any other. He enjoys playing in mud, burying himself in the sandbox, or rolling in the brambles as much as a dog of any other breed would. Grooming must be dealt with immediately.

The Pom will only stay healthy and looking like a Pom as long as you are willing to invest the time in keeping him that way. If you do not feel you have the time to do this yourself, it will be necessary to have a professional groomer do this for you. If you appreciate the look of the breed, realize it will take more than a little effort on your part to maintain it.

If you are willing to make the necessary commitment that a Pom requires, let us assure you there are few breeds that are more amiable or adaptable. While the Pom may well have been the pampered pet of nobility that spent the night tucked under the covers of an elegant bed, don't forget the Pom's early origins. The Pomeranian stands among the more rugged of the Toy breeds.

In the case of Pomeranians, the more, the merrier! The Pom has an outgoing personality and enjoys the company of other dogs.

The breed is basically a hardy one, and if purchased from a responsible breeder, is seldom prone to chronic illnesses. The Pom is of a diminutive size, but that does not mean he must be treated as if he's made of egg shells. For its size, the breed has amazing energy and strength. With proper instruction, children old enough to understand how to handle a small dog can learn to enjoy the exuberant personality of the Pom, and the Pom, in turn, will love the gentle child.

The breed is extremely playful and inquisitive. It is one that never ceases to find something to do. Yet a Pom is just as content to sit by your side when you read or listen to music. If introduced early enough and properly supervised, the Pom can coexist with your cat, rabbit, or even larger dog, as well as it can with humans. The Pom is a breed of which it can be said, without hesitation, that two dogs are just as easy to raise as one.

MALE OR FEMALE?

While the sex of a dog in many breeds is a very important consideration, this is not particularly the case with the Pom. The male Pom makes just as loving, devoted, and trainable a companion as the female. In fact, there are some that believe a male can be even more devoted to his master than a female.

It could be said that, in the case of the Pom, opposites seem to attract. My own males have appeared to develop a closer bond with me than my females. Males can be rather bold about being naughty at times, while the females are inclined to reserve their bad habits for those moments when you aren't looking.

Dedicated breeders are careful to be true to the Pomeranian's original type and purpose.

There is one important point to consider in determining your choice between male and female. While both must be trained not to relieve themselves in the home, males have a natural instinct to lift their leg and urinate to "mark" their home territory. It may seem confusing to many dog owners, but a male marking his home turf has absolutely nothing to do with whether or not he is housebroken. The two responses come from entirely different needs and must be dealt with in that manner. Some dogs are more difficult to train not to mark within the confines of the household than others. Males that are used for breeding are even more prone to this response and are harder to break of doing so.

On the other hand, females have their semiannual "heat" cycles once they reach sexual maturity. In the case of the female Pom, this can occur at any time, from as early as 6-8 months up to a year old. These cycles are accompanied by a vaginal discharge that creates the need to confine the female for about three weeks so that she does not soil her surroundings. It must be understood the female has no control over this bloody discharge, so it has nothing to do with training.

The Pomeranian is a devoted and energetic dog that makes a great pet and playmate for gentle children.

Although most Poms are not normally left outdoors unsupervised for long stretches of time, a female should not be outdoors unattended for even a brief moment or two during this period. The need for confinement and for keeping a careful watch over the female in heat is especially important in preventing her becoming pregnant by some neighborhood Lothario. Equally dangerous to her well-being is a male dog that is much larger than your female Pom. The dog may be too large to actually breed her, but he could seriously injure or even kill her in his attempts to do so.

Sexually related problems can be entirely eliminated by spaying the female and neutering the male. Unless a Pom has been purchased expressly for breeding or showing from a breeder capable of making this judgment, your dog should be sexually altered.

Breeding and raising puppies should be left in the hands of people who have the facilities to keep each puppy they breed until the correct home is found for him. This can often take many months after a litter is born. Most dog owners are not equipped for this. Naturally, a responsible Pom owner would never allow his or her pet to roam the streets or end his life in an animal shelter. Unfortunately, being forced to give a puppy away due to space or time constraints or to place him in a new home before thoroughly checking out the prospective buyer may, in fact, create this exact situation.

Breeders have often had parents ask to buy a female "just as a pet," but who really intend to breed the dog so that their children can witness "the birth process." There are countless books and videos now available that portray this wonderful event and do not add to the worldwide pet overpopulation we now face. Altering one's companion dogs not only precludes the potential of adding to this problem, it eliminates bothersome household problems and precautions.

It should be understood, however, that spaying and neutering are not reversible procedures. Spayed females or neutered males are not allowed to be shown in American Kennel Club shows, nor will altered animals ever be able to be used for breeding.

THE POMERANIAN PERSONALITY

Historically, the Pom has been a close companion to man. Whether he is the darling of royal courts or an international traveler, everything the Pom has done, he has done in the company of humans. He is happiest when allowed to continue that association. It simply would not do for a Pom to be shut away in a kennel or to have only occasional access to your life and environment. If this is your intent, you would be better served by another breed. The very essence of the Pom is in his unique personality and sensitive and loving nature, which are best developed by constant human contact.

Although the Pom is certainly not a vindictive breed, we are never surprised to hear that a completely housebroken Pom will suddenly forget all of his manners in protest of suddenly being left alone. Some Poms will let you know they are not getting the attention they need by destroying household items, particularly those things that belong to the individual that the dog is especially devoted to and is missing.

None of this should be construed to mean that only those people who are home to cater to every whim of their dog can be Pom owners. There are many working people who are away most of the day whose Poms are well mannered and trustworthy when left home alone. The key here seems to be the quality, not quantity, of time spent with their pet. Morning or evening walks, grooming sessions, game time, and simply having your Pom share your life when you are home is vital to the breed's personality development and attitude. A Pom likes to be talked to and praised. The old

Breeding should only be attempted by those with experience, knowledge, and the ability to care for the mother and the resulting offspring.

adage, "no man is an island," applies to dogs as well, particularly in the case of the Pom.

Everything about the Pom personality indicates it is a nonaggressive breed, but that does not mean the breed is shy or withdrawn. On the contrary, the Pom could well be considered the welcome wagon of the canine world! The Pom insists that there are no strangers in his life, and will even give special attention to those people who live an entire lifetime saying, "I don't like dogs!" In the company of a Pom, that attitude won't last very long.

Historically, the Pomeranian has been bred to be a companion to man and is happiest in the company of people.

We have never seen a Pom even indicate he would challenge his owner on any point, regardless of how much he might object to what he is being asked to do. A stern and disapproving voice is usually more than sufficient to let your dog know you disapprove of his behavior. It is never necessary to strike a Pom under any circumstance. A sharp "no!" is normally more than enough to make your point.

Within the confines of his own household, the Pom is an excellent watchdog in the sense that he will sound the alarm if he sees or hears anything unusual. Expect your Pom to let you know that the doorbell has rung or that someone is knocking.

A Pomeranian never loses sight of his Arctic, sled-dog heritage, and even though man's intervention has succeeded in reducing the breed's size, there has been little, if any, change in the amount of courage the little dog has. Although certainly not aggressive by any stretch of the imagination, the Pom won't back down from an intruder or another canine, regardless of size.

The Pom makes a great effort to please his owner and is highly trainable, as long as the trainer is not heavy-handed. Any training problems that are encountered are far more likely to be due to the owner's inexperience than the Pom's inability to understand what is to be learned. Although many Pom owners are inclined to think of their companions as "little people," it must be understood that the Pom is, first and foremost, a *dog*. Much like the wolves from which they are descended, dogs are pack animals and need a pack leader. Dogs are now totally dependent upon humans to provide that leadership and, when that leadership is not provided, can easily become confused and neurotic. Although small, remember that the Pom doesn't consider himself small at all and never lets size interfere with his acting and reacting like a regular-sized dog.

The Pomeranian makes a great effort to please his master and is highly trainable when offered guidance and discipline.

Setting boundaries is important for the well-being of your Pom and your relationship to him. The sooner your dog understands that there are rules that must be obeyed, the easier it will be for him to become an enjoyable companion. Once you learn to establish and enforce those rules, you will be able to determine how quickly this will come about. As mentioned earlier, the Pom is not vindictive or particularly stubborn, but he does need guidance in order to achieve his potential.

25

STANDARD for the Pomeranian

The AKC standard for the Pomeranian is written in simple, straightforward language that can be read and understood even by the beginning fancier. However, the standard's implications take many years to fully comprehend. This can only be accomplished by observing many quality Poms and reading as much about the breed as possible. Numerous books have been written about the breed, and it is well worth the Pom owner's time and effort to digest their contents if he is interested in showing or breeding his pet. Also, each country's standard is different.

There are some breeds that change drastically from puppyhood to adulthood. It would be extremely difficult for the untrained eye to determine the actual breed of some purebred dogs in puppyhood. This is not so with the Pom. Other than the length, texture, and color of the mature dog's coat, a Pom puppy will reflect in miniature what he will look like, in many respects, at maturity.

Can. Am. Ch. Moreno's Perri Winkle takes time out from a busy show career to be photographed with the judge that awarded him his blue ribbon.

It must be remembered that the breed standard describes a "perfect" Pom, but no dog is perfect and no Pom, not even the greatest dog show winner, will possess every quality asked for in the perfect form. It is how closely an individual dog adheres to the standard of the breed that determines his show potential.

One of the obvious traits that makes the Pom such an attractive dog is his beautiful double coat—a soft, plush undercoat with long, harsher guard hairs. A good part of the breed's appeal also comes from his fearless and dynamic temperament. While gentle, the breed is lively and playful, and one look into the sparkling black eyes of the Pom tells you that the breed is also capable of being entirely mischievous.

Size is very significant to the breed because the Pom is a lap-sized, Toy dog. The average weight of a Pomeranian is three to seven pounds. In addition, the Pom is beautifully balanced. Although small, he is never ungainly or clumsy in appearance.

The body is compact, with an overall look of elegance and agility.

There is absolutely no reason for the Pom to be unsound just because it is a Toy breed. The standard's requirements reveal well-made limbs, an easy, graceful way of moving, and balanced construction. Since the breed standard describes very normal construction and does not call for any unusual features, there should be no physical abnormalities.

AKC STANDARD FOR THE POMERANIAN

General Appearance—The Pomeranian in build and appearance is a cobby, balanced, short-coupled dog. He exhibits great intelligence in his expression and is alert in character and deportment.

Size, Proportion, Substance—*Size*—The weight of the Pomeranian for exhibition is from three to seven pounds. The ideal size for show specimens is four to five pounds. *Proportion*—The Pomeranian build and appearance is a cobby, balanced, short-coupled dog. The legs are of medium length in proportion to a well-balanced frame. *Substance*—The body is well ribbed and rounded. The brisket is fairly deep and not too wide.

Head—*Head* well proportioned to the body, wedge-shaped, with a fox-like expression. *Eyes* bright, dark in color, medium in size, almond-shaped and not set too wide apart or close together. Pigmentation around eye rims must be black, except self-colored in brown and blue. *Ears* small, carried erect, mounted high on the head and placed not too far apart. *Skull* not domed in outline. A round, domey skull is a *major fault*. *Muzzle*—There is a pronounced *stop*, with a rather fine but not snipy muzzle. Pigment around lips must be black, except self-colored in brown and blue. *Nose*—Pigmentation on the nose must be black, except self-colored in brown and blue. *Bite*—The teeth meet in a scissors bite, in which part of the inner surface of the upper teeth meets and engages part of the outer surface of the lower teeth. One tooth out of line does not mean an undershot or overshot mouth. An undershot mouth is a *major fault*.

Neck, Topline, Body—*Neck*—The neck is rather short, its base set well back on the shoulders. *Topline* is level. *Body*—The body is cobby, being well ribbed and rounded. *Chest*—The brisket is fairly deep and not too wide. *Tail*—The tail is characteristic of the breed. It turns over the back and is carried flat, set high.

Forequarters–*Shoulders*–The Pom is not straight in shoulder, but has sufficient layback of shoulders to carry the neck proudly and high. *Forelegs*–The forelegs are straight and parallel, of medium length in proportion to a well-balanced frame. *Pasterns*–The Pomeranian stands well up on toes. Down in pasterns is a *major fault*. Dewclaws on the forelegs may be removed. *Feet*–The Pomeranian stands well up on toes.

Hindquarters–*Legs*–The hocks are perpendicular to the ground, parallel to each other from hock to heel, and turning neither in nor out. Cow-hocks or lack of soundness in hind legs or stifles are *major faults*. Dewclaws, if any, on the hind legs are generally removed. *Feet*–The Pomeranian stands well up on toes.

Coat–*Body Coat*–Double-coated; a short, soft, thick undercoat, with

Even though the Pomeranian is a Toy breed, he still must possess the same soundness and structure as any other dog. Moreno's Tiny Tim By Choice, owned by author Julie Moreno.

longer, coarse, glistening outercoat consisting of guard hairs that must be harsh to the touch in order to give the proper texture for the coat to form a frill of profuse, standing-off straight hair. A soft, flat, or open coat is a *major fault*. *Tail Coat*—It is profusely covered with hair. *Leg Coat*—The front legs are well feathered and the hindquarters are clad with long hair or feathering from the top of the rump to the hocks. *Trimming*—Trimming for neatness is permissible around the feet and up the back of the legs to the first joint; trimming of unruly hairs on the edges of the ears and around the anus is also permitted. Overtrimming (beyond the location and amount described in the breed standard) should be *heavily penalized*.

The Pomeranian is a cobby, balanced dog whose expression displays great intelligence and alertness.

Color—*Classifications*—The Open Classes at Specialty shows may be divided by color as follows: Open Red, Orange, Cream & Sable; Open Black, Brown & Blue; Open Any Other Allowed Color. Acceptable colors to be judged on an equal basis. Any solid color, any solid color with lighter or darker shadings of the same color, any solid color with sable or black shadings, parti-color, sable, and black & tan.

The Pomeranian is shown in many different colors, including red, orange, cream, black, sable, brown, and blue. This black Pom proudly shows off his beautiful coat.

Black & tan is black with tan or rust, sharply defined, appearing above each eye and on the muzzle, throat, and forechest, on all legs and feet, and below the tail. Parti-color is white with any other color distributed in even patches on the body and a white blaze on the head. A white chest, foot, or leg on a whole-colored dog (except white) is a *major fault.*

Gait—The Pomeranian moves with a smooth, free, but not loose action. He does not elbow out in front or move excessively wide or cow-hocked behind. He is sound in action.

Temperament—He exhibits great intelligence in his expression and is alert in character and deportment.

Approved December 9, 1996
Effective January 31, 1997

31

SELECTING the Right Pomeranian for You

The Pom you buy will live with you for many years to come. It is not the least bit unusual for the well-bred Pom to live as long as 10, 12, or even 15 years. Obviously, it is important that the Pom you select has the advantage of beginning life in a healthy environment and coming from sound, healthy stock.

The only way you can be assured of this is to go directly to a breeder who has earned a reputation over the years for consistently producing Poms that are mentally and physically sound. A breeder will only earn this reputation by having a well-planned breeding program that has been governed by rigid selectivity. Selective breeding programs are aimed at maintaining the Pom's many fine qualities and eliminating any genetic weaknesses.

It is important that the Pomeranian puppy you select has all the advantages of coming from a sound healthy stock.

This process is both time-consuming and costly for a breeder, but it ensures the buyer of getting a dog that will be a joy to own. Responsible Pom breeders protect their investment by basing their breeding programs on the healthiest, most representative stock available and providing each succeeding generation with the very best care and nutrition.

The governing kennel clubs in the different countries of the world maintain lists of local breed clubs and breeders that can lead a prospective Pom buyer to responsible breeders of quality stock. If you are not sure how to contact an established Pom breeder in your area, contact the American Pomeranian Club, Inc., American Kennel Club, the United Kennel Club, or the Kennel Club in you own country for recommendations.

There are many well-intentioned pet shop owners who offer purebred puppies for sale. Unfortunately, most of the dogs offered by these shops come from distant kennels. The shop owner seldom has any real knowledge of the puppy's background or the kind of care he received during the critical period from birth to the time he arrived at the shop.

It is very likely that you will be able to find an established Pom breeder in your own area. If so, you will be able to visit the breeder, inspect the premises, and in many cases, see a puppy's parents and other relatives. These breeders are always willing to discuss any problems that might exist in the breed and how they should be dealt with. If there aren't any breeders in your immediate area, you can arrange to have a puppy shipped to you. There are breeders throughout the country who have shipped puppies to satisfied owners out-of-state and even to other countries.

Never hesitate to ask the breeder you visit or deal with any questions or to voice any concerns you might have relative to owning a Pom. You should expect the breeder to ask you a good number of questions, as well. Good breeders are just as interested in placing their puppies in a loving and safe environment as you are in obtaining a happy, healthy puppy.

A good Pom breeder will want to know if there are young children in the family, what their ages are, and if you or your children have ever owned a dog before. The breeder will also want to know if you live in an apartment or in a house. If you live in a house, he will want to know if you have a fenced yard and whether or not someone will be home during the day to attend to a young puppy's needs.

Few Pomeranian breeders maintain large kennels. In fact, you will find that many good Poms come from the homes of small hobby breeders who keep a few dogs and only have litters occasionally. The names of these people are just as likely to appear on the lists of recommended breeders from kennel clubs as the larger kennels that maintain many dogs. Hobby breeders are among the most dedicated to breeding quality Poms and have the distinct advantage of being able to raise their puppies in a home environment, with all of the accompanying personal attention and socialization so necessary to the breed.

Again, it is important that both the buyer and the seller ask questions. We would be highly suspect of a person who is willing to sell you a Pom puppy with no questions asked.

RECOGNIZING A HEALTHY PUPPY

Most Pom breeders will keep their puppies until they are at least 10 weeks old and have been given some of their initial puppy inoculations. By the time the litter is eight weeks old, it is entirely weaned, and no longer nursing on its mother. While the puppies are nursing, they have at least partial immunity from infectious diseases from their mother. However, once they stop nursing, they become highly susceptible to numerous diseases, many of which can be transmitted on the hands and clothing of humans. Therefore, it is extremely important that your puppy receives all the shots required for his age group.

SELECTING A PUPPY

A healthy Pom puppy is a bouncy, playful extrovert. Never select a puppy that appears shy or listless because you feel sorry for him. Doing so will undoubtedly lead to heartache and expensive veterinary costs. Do not attempt to make up for what the breeder lacked in providing proper care and nutrition. It seldom works.

The puppy you choose should have bright eyes and a healthy coat and should look clean and well taken care of.

Ask the breeder to help you select the puppy that would be best for you. Not all puppies have the same temperament—some are softer and more

reserved than others and need a quiet, gentle owner; others are far more boisterous and can handle a more active household.

If at all possible, ask the breeder if you can take the Pom puppy you are attracted to into a different room of the kennel or house. The smells will remain the same for the puppy, so he should still feel secure. Doing this gives you an opportunity to see how the puppy acts away from his littermates and allows you to inspect the puppy more closely.

Do understand that Pom puppies love their homes and their littermates. Not every puppy is going to be delighted when a stranger with totally foreign smells scoops him up and holds him. Discuss any temperament questions you might have with the breeder.

Even though Pom puppies are very small, they should feel sturdy to the touch. They should not feel bony, nor should their abdomens be bloated or extended. A puppy that has just eaten may have a full belly, but should never appear obese.

The insides of a healthy puppy's ears will be pink and clean. Dark discharge or a bad odor could indicate ear mites, a sure sign of lack of cleanliness and poor maintenance. A Pom puppy's breath should always smell sweet. His teeth must be clean and bright, and there should never be any malformation of the jaw, lips, or nostrils.

Pom eyes are dark and clear. Runny or irritated eyes could be caused by a myriad of problems—anything from dust and allergies to hairs irritating the eye itself. Again, talk to the breeder if you have questions about this.

Coughing or diarrhea are danger signals, as are any discharges from the nose or eruptions on the skin. The skin should be clean and the coat soft, clean, and lustrous.

Sound conformation can be determined at eight or ten weeks of age. The puppy's legs should be straight, without bumps or malformations. The toes should point straight ahead.

The puppy's attitude tells you a great deal about his state of health. Puppies that are feeling "out of sorts" won't react very quickly and will usually find a warm littermate to snuggle up to, preferring to stay that way even when the rest of the gang is playing or a human friend is available. The Pom is an extrovert. Do not settle for anything less in selecting your puppy.

SELECTING A SHOW-PROSPECT PUPPY

If you or your family are considering a show career for your puppy, we strongly advise putting yourself in the hands of an established breeder who has earned a reputation for breeding winning show dogs. They and they alone are the most capable of anticipating what one might expect from a young puppy of their line as he develops and reaches maturity.

Although the potential buyer should read their country's Kennel Club standard of perfection for the Pom, it is hard for the novice to really understand the nuances of what is asked for. The experienced breeder is best equipped to do this and will be only too happy to assist you in your quest. Even at that, no one can make accurate predictions or offer guarantees on a very young puppy.

Be sure that you do all your homework and learn all you can about the breed before taking a Pomeranian home.

Any predictions a breeder may make are based on his past experience with litters that produced winning show dogs. It should be obvious that the more successful a breeder has been in producing winning Poms over the years, the broader his basis for comparison will be.

The most any responsible breeder will say about a 12-week-old puppy is that he has "show potential." If you are serious about showing your Pom, it is strongly suggested that you wait until a puppy is 5 to 12 months old before making any decisions. It makes sense to assume that the older the puppy is, the easier it will be to determine how he will turn out.

Adulthood will bring an entirely new look to the Pom. His puppy fluff changes texture, and his coat can change color significantly. A good clue to guessing the final color is to look right behind the puppy's ears. Especially with reds and oranges, the color that you see there is usually the color the coat will be a maturity.

The Pomeranian's coat will go through different stages and colors before he reaches maturity. By the time he is 18 months old, his coat should reach its final stage.

There are actually three coat stages for a Pom: The first stage is a fluffy, puppy coat. This is followed by what is called the first juvenile coat, which he gets after his first three to five month shedding. Some puppies skip this second shedding stage and go right into the third stage, a mature coat that develops at about 14 to 18 months. This is the kind of coat that the Pom will have for the rest of his life.

Permanent teeth come in at six months of age and, until that time, "bites" (how the teeth are aligned) are uncertain. What look like proper-size teeth for a show Pom at three months can change drastically by the time the puppy matures.

The main consideration in determining potential is typical temperament, followed by correct type. Without these two characteristics, you simply do not have a Pomeranian.

There are many other beauty-point shortcomings a Pom puppy might have that would in no way interfere with your dog being a wonderful companion, but these faults would be serious drawbacks in the show ring. If you plan to breed your Pom, his pedigree is also very important. A pedigree of top winners and producers is far more apt to produce a Pom capable of winning and producing than a pedigree made up of mediocre dogs that have accomplished nothing in either respect. However, all breeders know that championship titles are not what produces outstanding quality. Careful breeding of carefully selected individuals is the key.

By using only the best quality dogs, breeders ensure that good temperament and health is passed down from generation to generation.

Many of the flaws in conformation and breeding are such that a beginner in the breed would hardly notice. Certainly, the novice would not know which of the dogs in a pedigree are outstanding and which are not.

Faults like one or no testicles for a male or an incorrect topline or tail set would not keep your Pom from being a happy, healthy, and loving companion, but would prevent him from being a winner in the show ring. This is why employing the assistance of a good breeder is so important. Nevertheless, the prospective buyer should be at least generally aware of what the Pom show puppy should look like.

All of the criteria regarding the soundness and health of a pet puppy apply to the show puppy as well. The show prospect must not only be sound and healthy, he must adhere to the standard of the breed very closely.

The complete standard of the breed appears in this book, and there are also a number of other books that can assist the newcomer in learning more about the Pom. The more you know about the history and origin of the breed, the better equipped you will be to see the differences that distinguish the show dog from the pet.

Like the pet, a show-prospect puppy must have a happy, outgoing temperament. He will be a compact little bundle of energy, which in most cases never seems to appear out of balance. However, there are some bloodlines that do experience an awkward stage. If this seems to be the condition of a puppy you are considering, be sure to mention it to the breeder. The show puppy will move around with ease and an "I-love-the-world" attitude. Temperament of this kind is a hallmark of the breed.

A small puppy is a lot of responsibility. A Pom puppy will take up a lot of your time and require plenty of care and attention.

PUPPY OR ADULT?

For the person anticipating a show career for their Pom or for someone hoping to become a breeder, the purchase of a young adult provides greater certainty with respect to quality. Even those who simply want a companion should consider the adult dog.

From a breeder's point of view, Poms act like puppies their entire lives and adapt to new places and people quite easily. Again, temperaments vary somewhat, so some of the maturing boy and girl dogs develop a slightly more sophisticated attitude.

In some instances, breeders will have males or females they no longer wish to use for breeding and, after the dogs have been altered, would prefer to have them live out their lives in a private home with all its attendant care and attention. In the private home environment, the dog will become the "one and only" instead of "one of many."

Acquiring an adult dog eliminates many of the problems involved in raising a puppy, and Poms, unlike some other breeds, do transfer well. They love to be with people, and although many of us hate to admit it, most Poms will be just as content living with one person as they are with another, as long as they are loved and well cared for.

Your Pom pup will have a good head start in life if his parents are healthy and well adjusted. Try to see the parents of the pup that you are considering.

Elderly people often prefer the adult dog, particularly one that is housebroken, because they are easier to manage and require less supervision and damage control. Adult Poms are seldom chewers and are usually more than ready to adapt to household rules.

There are other things to consider, though. Adult dogs have usually developed behaviors that may or may not fit into your routine. If a Pom has never been exposed to small children, the dog may be totally perplexed and often frightened by this new experience. Children are also inclined to be more active and vocal than the average adult, and this could intimidate the dog as well.

It is strongly advised that an adult dog be taken on a trial basis to see if the dog will adapt to the new owner's lifestyle and environment. Most often this works, but on rare occasions a prospective owner changes his mind and decides that training his or her dog from puppyhood will be worth the time and effort it requires.

IMPORTANT PAPERS

The purchase of any purebred dog entitles you to four very important documents: a health record, which includes an inoculation or "shot" record, a copy of the dog's pedigree, a registration certificate, and a health guarantee.

Inoculations

You will find that responsible Pom breeders have initiated the necessary preliminary inoculation series for their puppies by the time they are ready to leave home. These inoculations temporarily protect the puppies against hepatitis, leptospirosis, distemper, and canine parvovirus. "Permanent" inoculations will follow at a prescribed time. Because different breeders and

The breeder that you purchase your Pom from should provide you with an up-to-date list of the puppy's inoculations.

If you do not have the time or the inclination to train a puppy, an adult dog may be the right choice for you.

veterinarians take different approaches to inoculation, it is extremely important that the health record you obtain for your puppy accurately lists which shots have been given and when. In this way, the veterinarian you choose will be able to continue with the appropriate inoculation series as needed. In most cases, rabies inoculations are not given until a puppy is six months of age or older.

Pedigree

The pedigree is your dog's family tree. The breeder must supply you with a copy of a document authenticating your puppy's ancestors as far back as the third generation. All purebred dogs have pedigrees. The pedigree in and of itself does not mean that your puppy is of show quality. All it means is that all of his ancestors were registered Pomeranians. They may all have been purely of pet quality. Unscrupulous puppy dealers often try to imply that a pedigree indicates that dogs that have one are of championship caliber. This is not true. Again, it simply tells that all of the dog's ancestors are purebred.

Registration Certificate

The registration certificate is the canine world's birth certificate. This document is issued by a country's governing kennel club. When you transfer the ownership of your Pom from the breeder's name to your own name, the transaction is entered on this certificate and, once mailed to the appropriate kennel club, it is permanently recorded in their computerized files.

Breeders will often hold the registration certificate for the brief trial period during which both seller and buyer become satisfied that the puppy and new owner are compatible. No good breeder wants his puppy to be in a home where this is not the case.

Today, most good breeders in the US consider it important to sell Poms purchased as pets with spay or neuter contracts. This means that registration will not be transferred to the new owner until veterinarian certification has been furnished to indicate the puppy or dog involved has been spayed or neutered. Breeders do this because they have determined that the individual dog is not a good candidate for breeding and want to ensure that no accidents occur.

Keep all of your dog's documents in a safe place, as you will need them when you visit your veterinarian or if you ever wish to breed or show your Pom. Keep the name, address, and phone number of the breeder from whom you purchase your Pom in a separate place as well. If you ever lose any of these important documents, you will be able to contact the breeder to ask about obtaining duplicates.

Health and Suitability Guarantee

Any reputable breeder is more than willing to supply a written agreement that the purchase of your Pom is contingent upon his passing a veterinarian's examination within 48 hours. Ideally, you should be able to arrange an appointment with your chosen veterinarian right after you have picked up your puppy from the breeder and before you take the puppy home. If this is not possible, you should not delay this procedure any longer than the time specified in the health guarantee.

Some breeders prefer to have their dogs go into new homes for a trial period of about 48 hours to see if the arrangement is suitable for both dog and new owner. There are usually time restrictions involved, as well as monetary issues to be considered in arrangements of this kind.

A returned dog or puppy will normally be taken to a veterinarian to ensure the breeder that nothing has happened to the dog while he was away from his or her premises. The purchaser should expect costs of this nature to be deducted from the amount originally given to the seller. However, all details should be discussed, agreed upon, and put in writing before the buyer leaves the seller's home.

A reputable breeder will offer you a guarantee that the puppy you choose is healthy. Take your new puppy to the veterinarian within 48 hours of acquiring him.

DIET SHEET

Your Pom is the happy, healthy puppy he is because the breeder has been carefully

feeding and caring for him. Every breeder has his own particular regimen. Most breeders give the new owner a written record that details the amount and kind of food a puppy has been receiving. Follow these recommendations to the letter, at least for the first month or two after the puppy comes to live with you.

The diet sheet should indicate the number of times a day your Pom is accustomed to being fed and the kind of vitamin supplementation, if any, he receives. Following the prescribed procedure will reduce the chance of upset stomach and loose stools.

Breeders will normally give the new owner a small amount of prepared food, so that there are no changes the first day. In fact, we recommend using water from melted ice cubes for the puppy's drinking water. Although we have never been able to determine why, this seems to help prevent digestive problems during those first transfer days.

Usually, a breeder's diet sheet projects the increase and change in food that will be required as your puppy grows from week to week. If the sheet does not include this information, ask the breeder for suggestions regarding increases and the eventual change to adult food.

In the unlikely event that you are not supplied with a diet sheet by the breeder and are unable to get one, your veterinarian will be able to advise you. There are countless foods now being expressly manufactured to meet the nutritional needs of puppies and growing dogs. A trip down the pet aisle at your supermarket will prove just how many choices you have. Two important tips to consider: Read labels carefully for content and choose established, reliable manufacturers because you are more likely to get what you pay for. Feeding and nutrition are discussed later in the book.

TEMPERAMENT AND SOCIALIZATION

Temperament is both hereditary and environmental. Inherited good temperament can be ruined by poor treatment and a lack of proper socialization. A Pom puppy that comes from shy, nervous, or aggressive stock, or one that exhibits those characteristics himself will make a poor companion or show dog and should certainly never be bred. Therefore, it is critical that you obtain a happy puppy from a breeder who is determined to produce good temperaments and has taken all of the necessary steps to provide early socialization.

Temperaments in the same litter can range from confident and outgoing to shy and fearful, but, by and large, Pom temperament is and should be delightful. As stated previously, this temperament is a hallmark of the breed.

The Pom is not a particularly good breed for very young children. Through no fault of their own, toddlers are not usually able to understand that something as small as a Pom must be handled with care. A puppy must never be dropped, squeezed hard, or left unsupervised in an area where he can jump off of high things or have a door close on him.

The breeder will have started your Pom on the road to good nutrition, so stick to this original diet when you first get him home.

Ask the breeder to show everyone in your family the proper way to pick up and hold a Pom puppy. Knowing this will help you to avoid dropping or otherwise injuring a squirming puppy.

If you are fortunate enough to have older children in the household who are of an age capable of understanding a Pom puppy's needs, your socialization task will be assisted considerably. Poms raised with responsible children are the best pets. The two seem to understand each other and, in some way known only to the puppies and children themselves, they give each other the confidence to face the trying ordeal of growing up.

Every visitor that enters your household should be introduced to your dog. However, in the case of a Pom, this is usually completely unnecessary because your puppy will take care of those formalities on his own.

Once he has had all of his necessary inoculations, your puppy should go everywhere with you—the post office, the

market, the shopping mall—wherever. Be prepared to create a stir wherever you go, because what attracted you to the first Pom you met applies to other people as well. Everyone will want to pet your little companion, and there is nothing in the world better for him than getting attention.

If your puppy backs off from a stranger, pick him up and hand him to the person. The young Pom will quickly learn that all humans—young, old, short, or tall—are friends. You are in charge. You must call the shots.

If your Pom has a show career in his future, there are things in addition to being handled that he will have to be taught. All show dogs must learn to have their mouth and teeth inspected by a judge. Males must become accustomed to having their testicles touched because the judge at the dog show must determine that all male dogs are "complete," which means there are two normal-sized testicles in the scrotum. These inspections must begin during puppyhood and should be continued on a regular basis.

Poms seem to be entirely compatible with other dogs, as well as with humans. Interaction with larger dogs must be carefully supervised, however, because dogs are not aware of their own strength and can get entirely carried away in their enthusiasm to play. A Pom can incite his larger canine friend to romp and play in a manner that may well result in an unintentional accident.

As mentioned previously, the Pom has no idea that he is not a match for a Great Dane or St. Bernard and will not back down in the event of an altercation. If it is a big dog–little dog situation, careful supervision is needed until the new owner is absolutely positive the two can be trusted with each other.

The Adolescent Pomeranian

As described previously, the Pom's coat changes as the puppy begins to mature. When this happens, matting may occur where new hair growth meets already existing hair. While this does not always happen, some dogs are more prone to it than others. Thorough brushing during this time will only

Take your Pomeranian with you wherever you go. The more people he meets, the better socialized he will become.

49

take a few minutes and should be done every day to keep the coat's condition healthy and mat free.

It is important that you attend to these grooming sessions regularly during the early months of your puppy's growth. If your Pom has been groomed on a regular basis as a puppy, you will find that the task is much easier when you are working with a more abundant adult coat. More detailed grooming instructions are given later in the book.

Food needs will change during this growth period. Some Poms seem as if they can never get enough to eat, while others eat just enough to avoid starving. Think of Pom puppies as being as individualistic as children and act accordingly.

The amount of food you give your Pom should be adjusted to how much he will readily consume at each meal. If the entire meal is eaten quickly, add a small amount to the next feeding and continue to do so as the need increases. This method will ensure that you are giving your puppy enough food. However, you must also pay close attention to the dog's appearance and condition, because you do not want a puppy to become overweight or obese. On the other hand, watch the finicky puppy very closely.

Although temperament and personality remain somewhat consistent within a breed, every Pomeranian is an individual and should be treated as such.

The amount of food you give your Pom will need to be adjusted as he matures and develops.

Poms do not have as large a capacity to eat as some of the other breeds and can go down in weight very quickly.

At eight weeks of age, a Pom puppy is eating four meals a day. By the time he is six months old, the puppy can do well on two meals a day, with perhaps a snack in the middle of the day. If your puppy does not eat the food he's offered, he is either not hungry or not well. Your dog will always eat when he is hungry. If you suspect the dog is ill, a trip to the veterinarian is immediately in order.

The adolescent period is a particularly important one because it is the time your Pom must learn all of the household and social rules by which he will live for the rest of his life. Your patience and commitment during this time will not only produce a respected canine good citizen, but will forge a bond between the two of you that will grow into a wonderful relationship.

CARING for Your Pomeranian

FEEDING AND NUTRITION

The best way to make sure your Pom puppy is obtaining the proper amount and correct type of food for his age is to follow the diet sheet provided by the breeder. You will be less apt to run into digestive problems and diarrhea if you do not change the puppy's diet. Diarrhea is especially serious in young puppies the size of Poms. They can dehydrate very rapidly, causing severe problems and even death.

If it is necessary to change your Pom puppy's diet for any reason, it should be done gradually, over a period of several meals and a few days. Begin by adding a teaspoon or two of the new food, gradually increasing the amount until the meal consists entirely of the new product.

It is important to feed your Pomeranian a well-balanced and nutritious diet to keep him healthy.

By the time your Pom is 10 to 12 months old, you can reduce feedings to twice a day. The main meal can be given either in the morning or evening. It is really a matter of choice on your part. Feeding your dog in the morning ensures that even if you are held up on an evening errand, your dog will have already eaten once that day.

There are two important things to remember: Feed your dog the main meal at the same time every day, and make sure what you feed him is nutritionally complete.

The single meal can be supplemented by a midday snack of hard dog biscuits made especially for small dogs. These biscuits not only become highly anticipated treats to your Pom, but are genuinely helpful in maintaining healthy gums and teeth.

Make sure your Pomeranian has cool, clean water available to him at all times.

Balanced Diets

In order for a canine diet to qualify as "complete and balanced" in the United States, it must meet standards set by the Subcommittee on Canine Nutrition of the National Research Council of the National Academy of Sciences. Most commercial foods manufactured for dogs meet these standards and prove this by listing the ingredients contained in the food on every package or can. The ingredients are listed in descending order, with the main ingredient listed first. But always check with your breeder before changing to a different food than what your Pom has been fed. Some Poms can have extreme reactions to new foods.

Fed with any regularity at all, refined sugars can cause your Pom to become obese and will definitely create tooth decay. Early loss of teeth is common among Toy breeds, and there is

Nutritious treats can be healthy additions to your Pomeranian's diet, as well as a highly anticipated reward in training sessions. certainly no value in accelerating the process. Candy stores do not exist in nature, and canine teeth are not genetically disposed to handling sugars. Do not feed your Pom candy or sweets, and avoid products that contain sugar to any high degree.

Fresh water and a properly prepared, balanced diet that contains the essential nutrients in correct proportions are all a healthy Pom needs to be offered. Dog foods come canned, dry, semi-moist, "scientifically fortified," and "all-natural." A visit to your local supermarket or pet store will reveal how vast an array you will be able to select from.

It is important to remember that all dogs, whether toy or giant, are omnivores. While the vegetable content of the Pom diet should not be overlooked, a dog's physiology and anatomy are based on mostly carnivorous food acquisition. Protein and fat are absolutely essential to the well-being of your Pom. In fact, it is wise to add a few drops of vegetable oil or bacon drippings to your dog's diet, particularly during the winter months in colder climates.

Read the list of ingredients on the label of the dog food you buy. Animal protein should appear first on the list. A base of quality kibble to which meat and even table scraps have been added can provide a nutritious meal for your Pom.

Puppies receive all their nutrients from their mother in the first few weeks of life. Once weaned, however, they will look to you to fill all of their needs.

This having been said, it should be noted that in the wild, carnivores eat the entire beast they capture and kill. The carnivore's kills consist almost entirely of herbivores (plant-eating) animals. Invariably, the carnivore begins his meal with the contents of the herbivore's stomach, which provides the carbohydrates, minerals, and nutrients present in vegetables.

Through centuries of domestication, we have made our dogs entirely dependent upon us for their well-being. Therefore, we are responsible for duplicating the food balance that wild dogs find in nature. The domesticated dog's diet must include protein, carbohydrates, fats, roughage, and small amounts of essential minerals and vitamins.

Finding commercially prepared diets that contain all the necessary nutrients will not present a problem. It is important to understand, though, that some of these commercially prepared foods do not contain most of the nutrients your Pom requires. Most Pom breeders recommend vitamin supplementation for a healthy coat and increased stamina, especially for show dogs, pregnant bitches, or very young puppies, but only on the advice of a vet.

Oversupplementation

A great deal of controversy exists today regarding the orthopedic problems that afflict many breeds. Some experts claim that these problems are caused entirely by hereditary conditions, but many others feel that they can be exacerbated by overuse of mineral and vitamin supplements for puppies.

Feeding your dog in his crate can help him relax at mealtimes and prevent squabbles between your pets.

Oversupplementation is now looked upon by some breeders as a major contributor to numerous skeletal abnormalities found in the purebred dogs of the day. When giving vitamin supplementation, you should *never*

Proper nutrition is imperative to your dog's health. Veterinarians recommend elevated feeders to help reduce stress on your dog's neck and back muscles. The raised platform also provides better digestion while reducing bloating and gas. Photo courtesy of Pet Zone Products, Ltd.

exceed the prescribed amount. No vitamin, however, is a substitute for a nutritious, balanced diet.

Pregnant and lactating bitches do require supplementation of some kind, but here again, it is not a case of "if a little is good, a lot would be a great deal better." Extreme caution is advised, and it is always best to discuss supplementation with your veterinarian.

A Pom that becomes accustomed to being hand fed from the table can quickly become a pest at mealtime. Also, dinner guests may find the pleading stare of your little Pom less than appealing when dinner is being served.

Dogs do not care if food looks like a hot dog or a piece of cheese. Truly nutritious dog foods are seldom manufactured to look like food that appeals to humans. Dogs only care about how food smells and tastes. It is highly doubtful that you will be eating your dog's food, so do not waste your money on these "looks-just-like" products. Along these lines, most of the moist or canned foods are not advisable for the adult Pomeranian. They do far better on dry kibble.

Special Diets

There are now a number of commercially prepared diets for dogs with special dietary needs. The overweight, underweight,

The Pomeranian should not be left outdoors in extreme temperatures and should always have food, water, and shelter available to him at all times when outside.

or geriatric dog can have his nutritional needs met, as can puppies and growing dogs. The calorie content of these foods is adjusted accordingly. With the correct amount of the right foods and the proper amount of exercise, your Pom should stay in top shape. Again, common sense must prevail. Too many calories will increase weight, fewer will reduce weight.

Occasionally, a young Pom going through his teething period will become a poor eater. The concerned owner's first response is to tempt the dog by hand feeding him special treats and foods that the problem eater seems to prefer. This practice only compounds the problem. Once the dog learns to play the waiting game, he will turn up his nose at anything other than his favorite food, knowing full well that what he *wants* to eat will eventually arrive.

Unlike humans, dogs do not have suicidal tendencies. A healthy dog will not starve himself to death. He may not eat enough to keep himself in the shape we find ideal and attractive, but he will definitely eat enough to maintain himself. If your

Pom is not eating properly and appears to be too thin, it is probably best to consult your veterinarian.

Exercise

If your own exercise proclivities lie closer to a walk around the block than to ten-mile marathon runs, your choice of a Pom was probably a wise one. The Pom is not a breed that requires taking your energy level to its outer limits. In fact, most Poms self exercise, if they are allowed the freedom to do so. If your Pom shares his life with children or another dog, he will undoubtedly get all of the exercise he needs to stay fit. A Pom is always ready for a romp or may even invent some new game that entails plenty of aerobic activity.

Although not particularly athletic, the Pom does possess a lot of energy and requires regular exercise for his physical and mental well-being.

This does not mean that your Pom will not benefit from a daily walk in the park or around the block. On the contrary, slow, steady exercise that keeps your companion's heart rate in the working area will help extend his life. If your Pom is doing all of this with you at his side, you are increasing the chances that the two of you will enjoy each other's company for many more years to come.

Naturally, common sense must be used in determining the frequency and intensity of the exercise you give your Pom. What you consider a fast walk could be going full-tilt for your Pom. Remember, young puppies have short bursts of energy and then require long rest periods. No puppy of any breed should be forced to accompany you on extended walks, because serious injuries can result. Again, short exercise periods and long rest stops are necessary for any Pom under 10 or 12 months of age. Most adult Poms, however, will willingly walk as far as the average owner is inclined to go.

Hot Weather

Caution must be exercised in hot weather. First, the Pom is not a breed that particularly enjoys being exposed to blazing, summer sun. Plan your walks for the first thing in the morning, if at all possible. If you cannot arrange to do this, wait until the sun has set and the outdoor temperature has dropped to a comfortable degree.

You must *never* leave your Pom in the car in hot weather. Temperatures can soar in a matter of minutes, and your dog can die of heat exhaustion in less time than you would ever imagine. Rolling down the windows helps very little and can be dangerous if an overheated Pom panics and attempts to escape through the open window. A word to the wise—leave your dog at home in a cool room on hot days.

Proper socialization with different people and places will ensure that your Pomeranian will be able to adjust to any situation.

The Pom should not be expected to endure extremely cold weather if he is not active. The breed is one of the hardier Toys, and most Poms will enjoy a good romp in the snow. However, never allow him to remain outdoors in the cold for extended periods, particularly, if he is sitting still or shivering. Nor should you allow your Pom to remain wet if the two of you get caught in the rain. At the very least, thoroughly towel-dry your wet Pom. Better still, use your blow drier (set on *medium*) to make sure your dog is completely dry and mat free.

Socialization

The Pom is, by nature, a happy dog and takes most situations in stride. However, it is important to accommodate the breed's natural instincts by making sure your dog is accustomed to everyday events of all kinds. Traffic, strange noises, loud or hyperactive children, and strange animals can be very intimidating to any dog that has never experienced them before. Gently and gradually introduce your puppy to as many strange situations as you possibly can.

Make it a practice to take your Pom with you everywhere whenever practical. The breed is a true crowd pleaser and you will find that your Pom will savor all the attention he gets.

GROOMING Your Pomeranian

O ften, what initially attracts people to the Pom is his sparkling, stand-off coat. Your Pom will only have that special look as long as you are diligent in keeping his coat thoroughly washed and brushed. You must either learn to do this yourself or find a reliable groomer.

A breeder has usually begun to train a Pom puppy to cooperate with grooming, and it is wise to learn to follow his technique. His advice on brushes, combs, and shampoos is invaluable. Don't forget that breeders have had a lot of experience in these areas.

The Pomeranian's beautiful, abundant coat gives him his distinctive appearance.

Good grooming cannot be accomplished with occasional attacks on a problem after long periods of neglect. The damage done by neglecting a Pom's coat may have to be corrected by shaving away the dog's entire coat because of the mats that may have developed. This is neither attractive, nor is it good for your dog. If you are not willing to put in the time and effort necessary to maintain the Pom's coat, get a smooth-coated dog instead.

PUPPY COAT

Undoubtedly, the breeder from whom you purchased your Pom will have begun to accustom the puppy to grooming as soon as he had enough hair to brush. You must continue with grooming sessions or begin them at once if, for some reason, they have not been started. You and your Pom will spend many hours involved with this activity over a lifetime, so it is imperative that both of you learn to cooperate in the endeavor to make it an easy and pleasant experience.

If you admire the fluffy, well groomed look of show dogs, you should consider using a hair dryer on your dog for after his bath. Start using it when he's a pup so he will learn to enjoy the experience. Photo courtesy of Metropolitan Vacuum Cleaner Co., Inc.

The first piece of equipment you should obtain is a grooming table, which can be built or purchased at your local pet emporium or pet good supplier. Even a sturdy snack table topped with a nonskid pad can be used, as long as it is steady. A wobbly table is very frightening for any dog. Make sure that the table you use is a comfortable height to work at.

You will also need to invest in two brushes, a steel comb, barber's scissors, and a pair of nail clippers. Also very useful is a good-quality, spray-type coat conditioner. Considering the fact that you will be using these grooming tools for many years to come, it is recommended that you buy the best of these items you can afford.

The brush that you will need is called a pin brush, sometimes called a "Poodle brush." Another popular brush used is a "slicker brush." The slicker can severely break Pom hair and damage the coat if not used carefully. It is primarily used to help unsnarl mats and to run carefully through longer hair. These brushes, along with a fine-toothed comb, nail clippers, and coat conditioner can be purchased at your local pet shop or at any dog show.

Do not attempt to groom your puppy on the floor. The puppy will only try to get away from you when he has decided enough is enough, and you will spend a good part of your time chasing the puppy around the room. Sitting on the floor for long stretches of time is not the most comfortable position in the world for the average adult either.

The Pom puppy should be taught to lie on his side to be groomed. As your Pom grows and develops his adult coat, you will find the bit of effort you invested in teaching the puppy to do this will be time well spent as he will be kept in that position for most of the brushing process. Your Pom will also have to be kept in the standing position for his final brushing touches. You will finish grooming by brushing from rear to front, so that the coat is brushed toward the head.

Begin training by laying the puppy down on his side on the table. Speak reassuringly to the puppy as you stroke his head and rump. (This is a good time to practice the stay command.) Do this a number of times before you attempt to do any grooming. Repeat the process until your puppy understands what he is supposed to do when you place him on the grooming table.

To brush the puppy coat, start with the pin brush. When your Pom has developed his adult coat, you will only use the pin brush for overall grooming and your fine-toothed comb to help untangle mats.

Begin with your puppy lying on his side. You will start what is called "line brushing" at the top of the shoulder. Part the hair in a straight line, from the front of the shoulder, straight on down to the bottom of the chest. Brush through the hair to the right and left of the part. Mist the part with an antistatic spray or conditioner.

In order to care for the Pomeranian's signature double coat, you will need to acquire the proper grooming tools.

Never brush your Pom's coat dry—if nothing else is available, put some distilled water in a spray bottle and use it to moisten the coat before you brush. Start at the skin and brush out to the very end of the hair, but do this in a flipping rather than dragging motion. The latter will pull out the coat.

Brush a small section at a time and continue on down the part. When you reach the bottom of the part, return to the top and make another part just to the right of the first line you brushed. *Part, brush, and mist.* You will repeat this process, moving each part toward the rear until you reach the puppy's tail.

If you encounter a mat that does not brush out easily, use your fingers, the pin brush, and the steel comb to help separate the hairs as much as possible. Do not cut or pull out the matted hair. Apply some powder directly to the mat and brush completely from the skin out.

A grooming table will assist you in grooming your Pomeranian. This little beauty proudly shows off her well-cared-for coat.

If you can eliminate the tugging and tearing of your dog's coat in the detangling process, your dog will appreciate it, and his coat is less likely to be split or torn. Photo courtesy of Wahl, USA.

When you have finished brushing the puppy on one side, turn him over and complete the entire process on the other side—*part, brush, and spray.* As your Pom becomes accustomed to this process, you may find that he considers this nap time. You may have to lift your puppy into the standing position to arouse him from his slumber.

With the puppy standing, brush the chest and tail. Do this gently so as not to break the hair. When brushing on and around the rear legs, be sure to give special attention to the area of the anus and genitalia. Needless to say, it is important to be extremely careful when brushing in these areas, because they are very sensitive and easily injured. Again, with the puppy standing, the final strokes are all toward the head.

Nail Trimming

This is a good time to accustom your Pom to having his nails trimmed and feet inspected. Always inspect your dog's feet for cracked pads. If your Pom is allowed out in the yard or accompanies you to the park or woods, check between the toes for splinters and thorns. Pay particular attention to any swollen or tender areas. In many sections of the country, there is a weed called a "foxtail," which releases a small, hook-like barb that carries its seed. The hook easily finds its way into a dog's foot or between his toes and works its way deep into the dog's flesh. This will very quickly cause soreness and infection. These barbs should be removed by your veterinarian before serious problems result.

The nails of a Pom who spends most of his time indoors or on grass when outdoors can grow long very quickly. Do not allow the nails to become overgrown and then expect to cut them back easily. If you hear nails click on the floor, they are too long.

Your Pom must become accustomed to extensive grooming procedures if he is going to compete in dog shows.

Each nail has a blood vessel running through the center of it called the "quick." The quick grows close to the end of the nail and contains very sensitive nerve endings. If the nail is allowed to grow too long, it will be impossible to cut it back to a proper length without cutting into the quick. This causes the dog severe pain and can also result in a great deal of bleeding that can be difficult to stop.

If the quick is nipped during the trimming process, there are a number of blood-clotting products available at pet shops that will almost immediately stem the flow of blood. It is wise to have one of these products on hand in case there is a nail trimming accident or the dog tears a nail on his own.

GROOMING THE ADULT POMERANIAN

Ideally, you and your Pom have spent many months between puppyhood and full maturity learning to assist each other through the grooming process. Both of you have survived as the puppy coat changed and entirely different adult hair arrived. Fortunately, the correctly groomed Pom coat is not nearly as

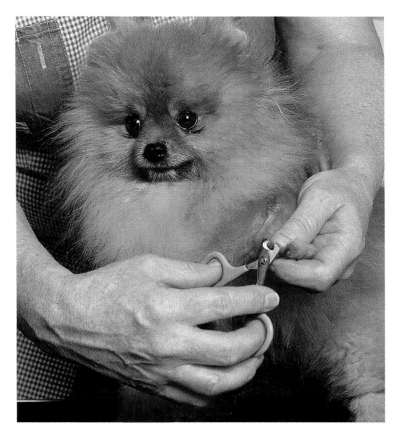

Never ignore your Pomeranian's nails and feet while grooming. Check for cracked footpads and keep his nails trimmed to prevent injuries.

difficult to take care of as the coats of many other breeds.

The method of brushing an adult coat is the same as that used when your Pom was a puppy. The only difference is that you have a bit more dog to groom and the hair itself is thicker.

While you might expect grooming an adult Pom to be a monumental task, this is not necessarily so. The important thing is consistency. A 15-minute session, every few days, precludes your dog's hair from becoming a tangled mess that may take hours to comb out. Then, too, you have been practicing the brushing routine for so long, it has undoubtedly become second nature to both of you.

Scissors can be used to remove hair that becomes frequently matted in "arm pits" (under the legs where they join the body) and under the dog's stomach.

BATHING

A Pom should never be bathed until he has been thoroughly brushed. If all mats are not removed before you bathe him, you will end up with a fused cotton ball! Mats will get worse when doused with water.

A small cotton ball placed inside each ear will prevent water from running down into the dog's ear canal, and a drop or two of mineral oil or a dab of petroleum jelly placed in each eye will preclude shampoo irritating the eyes.

Make sure you rinse your Pomeranian thoroughly after bathing him. Skin irritation can be caused by shampoo left in his coat.

A rubber mat should be placed at the bottom of the tub, so that your dog does not slip and become frightened. A rubber spray hose is absolutely necessary to remove all shampoo residue. Rinse thoroughly and rinse again.

In bathing, start behind the ears and work toward the back. Finally, carefully wash around the face, being very careful not to get suds in your dog's eyes. Rinse well. Shampoo residue in the coat is sure to dry out the hair and could cause skin irritation.

As soon as you have completed the bath, use a heavy towel to remove as much of the excess water as possible. Your Pom will undoubtedly assist you in the process by shaking a great deal of the water out of the coat on his own.

Using a Hair Dryer

It is very important to gently "brush-dry" your Pom using your pin brush and a hair dryer. Always set your hair dryer at the warm setting, never hot. The hot setting may be quicker, but it will also dry out the hair and could easily burn your Pom's delicate skin. Make sure the coat is *thoroughly* dry. A damp undercoat can create a myriad of skin problems, to say nothing of impossible matting.

Keep the ears clean by putting a little ear cleanser inside the ear and wiping it with a tissue. Do not probe into the ear beyond where you can see! The delicate ear drum can be easily injured. If you suspect a problem deeper in the ear canal, consult your veterinarian.

HOUSEBREAKING and Training Your Pomeranian

There is no breed of dog that cannot be trained. It does appear that some breeds are more difficult to get the desired response from than others. In many cases, however, this has more to do with the trainer and his training methods than the dog's inability to learn. With the proper approach, any dog that is not mentally deficient can be taught to be a good canine citizen. Many dog owners do not understand how a dog learns or realize that they should be breed-specific in their approach to training.

Young puppies have an amazing capacity to learn. This capacity is greater than most humans realize. It is important to remember, though, that these young puppies also forget quickly, unless they are reminded of what they have learned by continual reinforcement.

Young puppies have an amazing capacity to learn, and your eager-to-please Pomeranian will want to learn what you have to teach him.

As puppies leave the litter, they begin searching for two things: a pack leader and the rules set down by that leader. Because puppies,

Housebreaking your Pomeranian relies on your patience and consistent reinforcement.

particularly Pom puppies, are cuddly, cute, and very small, their owners fail miserably in supplying these very basic needs of every dog. Instead, the owner immediately begins to respond to the demands of the puppy.

For example, a puppy quickly discovers that he will be allowed into the house or a room because he is barking or whining, instead of learning that he can only enter the house when he is *not* barking or whining. Instead of learning that the only way he will be fed is to follow a set procedure (i.e., sitting or lying down on command), he learns that leaping about the kitchen or barking incessantly is what gets results.

If the young puppy cannot find his pack leader in an owner, he will assume the role of pack leader himself. As small as that bit of fluff is, the Pom puppy will learn to make his own rules if there are none imposed. Unfortunately, the negligent owner continually reinforces the puppy's decisions by allowing him to govern the household. With small dogs like our Pom, this scenario can produce a neurotic nuisance. In the case of large

Crate training is the fastest and easiest way to housebreak your Pomeranian, because dogs do not want to soil where they eat or sleep.

dogs, the situation can be downright dangerous. Neither situation is an acceptable one.

The key to successful training lies in establishing the proper relationship between dog and owner. The owner or owning family must be the pack leader and the individual or family must provide the rules by which the dog abides.

Once this is established, ease of training depends greatly on how much a dog needs his master's approval. The dependent dog lives to please his master and will do everything in his power to evoke the approval response from the person he is devoted to.

At the opposite end of the spectrum, we have the totally independent dog that is not remotely concerned with what his master thinks or wants. Dependency varies from one breed to the next and, to a degree, within breeds as well. Poms are no exception to this rule. Fortunately for the owner of a Pom, however, this breed really wants to please.

HOUSEBREAKING OR HOUSETRAINING

The Crate Method

If you are obedience training or housebreaking your Pom, a major key to success is *avoidance*. It is much easier for your Pom to learn a good habit than to unlearn a bad one. The crate training method of housebreaking is a highly successful way to avoid bad habits before they begin.

Be sure to provide your Pom puppy with plenty of positive reinforcement and praise when he does something right in the training process.

First-time dog owners are inclined to initially see the crate or cage method of housebreaking as cruel, but those same people will later thank us profusely for having suggested it in the first place. They are also surprised to find that the puppy will eventually come to think of his crate as a place of private retreat or a den where he will go for rest and privacy. The success of the crate method is based on the fact that puppies will not soil the area in which they sleep, unless they are forced to do so.

Use of a cage reduces housetraining time to an absolute minimum and avoids keeping a puppy under constant stress by incessantly correcting him for making mistakes in the house. The anticage advocates consider it cruel to confine a puppy for any length of time, but find no problem in constantly harassing and punishing the puppy because he has wet the carpet or relieved himself behind the sofa.

Crates come in a wide variety of styles. The fiberglass shipping kennels used by airlines are popular with many Pom owners, but residents of extremely warm climates sometimes prefer a wire cage. Both are available at pet stores.

The crate used for housebreaking should only be large enough for the puppy to stand up, lie down, and stretch out in comfortably. There are many sizes to choose from. We advise using the Number 100 size (small), airline-type crate. This size is ideal for most Poms.

Begin using the crate when you feed your Pom puppy his meals. Place him in the crate and keep the door closed and latched while the puppy is eating. When the meal is finished, open the cage and carry the puppy outdoors to the spot where you want him to learn to eliminate. In the event that you do not have or do not want to use outdoor access or if you will be away from home for extended periods of time, begin housebreaking by placing newspapers in an out-of-the-way corner that the puppy can easily get to. If you consistently take your puppy to the same spot, you will reinforce the habit of going there for that purpose.

Put your Pomeranian on a regular feeding schedule so you can anticipate when he will need to go outside.

It is important that you do not let the puppy loose after eating. Young puppies will eliminate almost immediately after eating or drinking. They will also be ready to relieve themselves when they first wake up and after playing. If you keep a watchful eye on your puppy, you will quickly learn when this is about to take place. A puppy usually circles and sniffs the floor just before he relieves himself. Do not give your puppy any opportunity to learn that he can eliminate in the house. Your housetraining chores will be reduced considerably if you prevent this from happening.

If you accustom your Pom to his crate at an early age, he will come to think of it as a cozy den in which to retreat and relax.

If you are unable to watch your puppy every minute, he should be in his crate, with the door securely latched. Each time you put your puppy in the crate, give him a small treat of some kind. Throw the treat to the back of the crate and encourage the puppy to walk in on his own. When he does so, praise him and perhaps hand him another piece of the treat through the opening in the front of the crate.

Do not succumb to your puppy's complaints about being in his crate. He must learn to stay there and to do so without unnecessary complaining. A quick "no" command and a tap on the crate will usually get the puppy to understand that

theatrics will not result in liberation. (Remember, as the pack leader, you make the rules, and the puppy wants to learn what they are.) Understand that a puppy that is 8 to 12 weeks old will not be able to contain himself for long periods of time. Puppies that age must relieve themselves every few hours, except at night. Your schedule must be adjusted accordingly. Also, make sure your puppy has relieved both his bowel and bladder the last thing at night and do not dawdle when you wake up in the morning.

Your first priority in the morning is to get the puppy outdoors. How early this ritual will take place will depend much more on your puppy than on you. If your Pom is like most others, there will be no doubt in your mind when he needs to be let out. You will also quickly learn to tell the difference between the "this is an emergency" complaint and the "I just want out" grumbling. Do not test the young puppy's ability to contain himself. His vocal demand to be let out is confirmation that the housebreaking lesson is being learned.

If you find it necessary to be away from home all day, you will not be able to leave your puppy in a crate. On the other hand, do not make the mistake of allowing him to roam the house, or even a large room, at will. Confine the puppy to a very small room or partitioned-off area and cover the floor with newspaper. If you leave the puppy in a small room, do not close the door. Use a partition or gate that the puppy can see through, and he will be far more apt to stay calm. Poms do not like to be shut away anywhere they cannot see out of.

Make this area large enough so that the puppy does not have to relieve himself next to his bed, food, or water bowls. You will soon find that the puppy will be inclined to use one particular spot to perform his bowel and bladder functions. When you are home, you must take the puppy to this exact spot to eliminate at the appropriate time.

Restricting your Pom to one safe area will help enforce housebreaking rules. Make sure to provide your dog with plenty of time outside to attend to his needs.

BASIC TRAINING

The state of your own emotions and the environment in which you train are just as important to your dog's training as his state of mind is at the time. Never begin training when you are irritated, distressed, or preoccupied. Also, you should not begin basic training in a place that interferes with your dog's or your concentration. Once the commands are understood and learned, you can begin testing your dog in public places. First, the two of you should work in a place where you can concentrate fully upon each other.

You must remain aware of the sensitivity level of your Pom and his desire to please. Poms respond well to lots of praise, but do not respond to yelling or being struck. Never resort to shaking or striking your Pom puppy. A very stern "No!" is usually more than sufficient and as extreme as you will ever need to be.

To an extent, the breed can be surprising. Several Pomeranians have achieved the American obedience title of Companion Dog Excellent (CDX) degrees. It is hard to go beyond that, due to the breed's small size, but the Pom has no idea he is not as capable as the most talented Rottweiler or Golden Retriever. The breed's ability to learn and perform far exceeds its size.

The No Command

There is no doubt whatsoever that one of the most important commands your Pom puppy will ever learn is the no command. It is critical that the puppy learns this command as soon as possible. One important piece of advice in using this and all other commands—never give a command you are not prepared and able to enforce! Always use the dog's name when you give the command—"No, Gamin, no!" "Gamin, come!" Using the puppy's name will get his attention immediately.

A good leader does not enforce rules arbitrarily. The only way a puppy learns to obey commands is to realize that once issued, commands must be complied with. Learning the no command should begin the first day of the puppy's arrival at your home.

Be fair to your dog. He can easily learn the difference between things he can and cannot do. However, a dog is not able to learn that there are some things he can do one day but not the next. Yelling at your dog for lying on the bed, when it was perfectly all right for him to do so the previous day will only confuse him.

Leash or Lead Training

Begin leash training by putting a soft, lightweight collar on your puppy. After a few hours of occasional scratching at the unfamiliar object, your puppy will quickly forget it is even there. The best collar to use is a soft, small cat collar. It will not crush the ruff area around the neck, which you will want to stand out full. Do not leave the collar on when you are not at home, however. There is a small loop on it that can easily get caught on something and harm the puppy.

It may not be necessary for the puppy or adult Pom to wear his collar and identification tags within the confines of your home, but no Pom should ever leave the house without wearing a collar and without the attached leash held securely in your hand. Some countries require dogs to be leashed at all times in public places

Begin getting your puppy accustomed to his collar by leaving it on him for a few minutes at a time. Gradually extend the time you leave the collar on. Once this is accomplished, attach a lightweight leash to the collar while you are playing with the puppy. Do not try to guide the puppy yet. At this point, you are only trying to get the puppy used to having something attached to the collar.

Training your Pomeranian to walk on a leash will make your daily walks much more enjoyable.

Get your puppy to follow you as you move around by coaxing him along with a treat of some kind. Let the puppy smell what you have in your hand and then move a few steps back holding the treat in front of the puppy's nose. Just as soon as the puppy takes a few steps toward you, praise him enthusiastically and continue to do so as you continue to move along.

Make the first few lessons brief and fun for the puppy. Continue the lessons in your home or yard until the puppy is completely unconcerned about the fact that he is on a leash. With a treat in one hand and a leash in the other, you can begin to guide the puppy in the direction you wish to go. Eventually, the two of you can venture out to the pavement in front of your house and then on to adventures everywhere. This is one lesson no puppy is too young to learn.

The Come Command

The next and most important lesson for the Pom puppy to learn is to come when he is called. Therefore, it is very important that the puppy learns his name as soon as possible. Constant repetition is what does the trick when teaching a dog his name. Use the name every time you talk to him. Talk to your dog? There is an amusing quotation that appeared in an old British dog book regarding conversations with our canine friends that says it all. It states simply, "Of course you should talk to your dogs. But talk sense!"

Learning to come on command could save your dog's life when the two of you venture out into the world. A dog needs to understand that he must obey the come command without question, but he should not associate the command with fear. Your dog's response to his name and the word "come" should always be associated with a pleasant experience, such as receiving great praise, being pet, or getting a food treat.

Again, remember it is much easier to avoid learning bad habits than it is to correct them once set. *Never* give the come command, unless you are sure your puppy will come to you.

The very young puppy is far more inclined to respond to the come command than the older dog would be. Young puppies are entirely dependent upon you. An older dog may lose some of that dependency and become preoccupied with his surroundings. Therefore, begin your come command training early on.

Initially, use the command when the puppy is already on his way to you or give the command while walking or running away from him. Clap your hands and sound excited about having your puppy join in on this "game."

The very young Pom puppy will normally want to stay as close to his owner as possible, especially in strange surroundings. When your puppy sees you moving away, his natural inclination will be to get close to you. This is a perfect time to use the come command.

You may want to attach a long leash or light rope to the puppy's collar to ensure the correct response. Do not chase or punish your dog for not obeying the come command. Doing so in the initial stages of training makes the puppy associate the command with something to fear, which will result in avoidance rather than the immediate positive response you desire. It is imperative that you praise your Pom puppy and give him a treat when he does come to you, even if he voluntarily delays responding for several minutes.

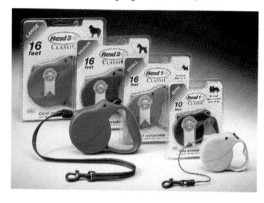

Retractable leashes provide dogs with freedom while allowing the owner complete control. Leashes are available in a wide variety of lengths for all breeds of dog. Photo courtesy of Flexi-USA, Inc.

The Sit and Stay Commands

Learning the sit and stay commands is as important to your Pom puppy's safety as the no command and learning to come when called. Even very young Poms can learn the sit command quickly, especially if it appears to be a game and a food treat is involved.

First, remember the Pom-in-training should always be on a collar and leash for all of his lessons. A Pom is curious about

Hand gestures in conjunction with verbal commands can be very effective when training your Pomeranian. This Pom obeys the hand signal for the stay command.

everything that goes on around him, and a puppy is not beyond getting up and walking away when he has decided he needs to investigate something.

Give the sit command just before reaching down and exerting, pressure on your puppy's rear. Praise the puppy profusely when he does sit, even though it was you who exerted the effort. A food treat of some kind always makes the experience more enjoyable for the puppy.

Continue holding the dog's rump down as you repeat the sit command several times. If your puppy makes an attempt to get up, repeat the command again, while exerting pressure on the rear end until the correct position is assumed. Make your puppy stay in this position a little bit longer with each succeeding lesson. Begin with a few seconds and increase the time as lessons progress over the following weeks.

If your puppy attempts to get up or to lie down, correct him by simply saying, "Sit!" in a firm voice. The command should be accompanied by returning him to the desired position. Your dog should get up only when you decide he should be allowed to do so. Do not test the extent of your Pom puppy's patience. Remember, you are dealing with a baby, and the attention span of any youngster is relatively limited. When you decide the dog can get up, call his name, and say "OK." Make a big fuss over him. Praise and a food treat are in order every time your Pom responds correctly.

Once your puppy has mastered the sit lesson, you may start training him to perform the stay command. With your Pom on leash and facing you, command him to sit, then take a step or two backward. If your dog attempts to get up to follow, firmly say, "Sit, stay!" While you are saying this, raise your hand, palm toward the dog, and again command, "Stay!"

The sit command is the foundation for all other commands because it teaches the dog self-control.

If your dog attempts to get up, you must correct him at once, returning him to the sit position and repeating the command, "Stay!" Once your Pom begins to understand what you want, you can gradually increase the distance you step back. With a long leash attached to your dog's collar, start with a few steps and gradually increase the distance to several yards. It is important for your Pom to learn that the sit/stay command must be obeyed no matter how far away you are. With advanced training, your Pom can be taught that the command must be obeyed, even when you leave the room or are entirely out of sight.

As your Pom becomes accustomed to responding to this and is able to remain in the sit position for as long as you command him to, do not end the verbal command by calling the dog to you. Walk back to your Pom and say, "OK." This will let your dog know that the command is over. When your Pom becomes entirely dependable in this lesson, it will be acceptable to begin calling the dog to you.

Teaching puppies the sit/stay command can take considerable time and patience. You must not forget that their attention span will be short. Keep the stay command part of the training very short until your puppy is about six or eight months old.

The Down Command

Do not try to teach your Pom puppy too many things at once. Wait until you have mastered one lesson quite well before moving on to something new.

When you feel confident that your puppy is comfortable with the sit and stay commands, you can start work on the down command. This is the single-word command for "lie down." Use the down command *only* when you want the dog to lie down. If you want your Pom to get off of your favorite chair or to stop jumping up on people, use the "off" command. Do not interchange these two commands. Doing so will only confuse your dog, after which evoking the right response will become next to impossible.

The down command may be a difficult one for your Pom to master, because the down position represents submission to your dog.

The down position is especially useful if you want your Pom to remain in one place for a long period of time. Most dogs are far more inclined to stay put when they are lying down than when they are sitting or standing.

Teaching your Pom this command may take more time and patience than the previous lessons the two of you have undertaken. Some animal behaviorists believe that assuming the down position somehow represents greater submissiveness.

With your Pom seated facing you, hold a treat in your right hand and the excess part of the leash in your left

With a treat in your hand, lead your Pomeranian's nose downward until he lies down. Praise him and give him the treat if he does what you ask.

hand. Hold the treat under the dog's nose and slowly bring your hand down to the ground. Your dog will follow the treat with his head and neck. As he does, give the down command and exert *light* pressure on the dog's shoulders with your left hand. If your dog resists the pressure on his shoulders, *do not continue pushing down*. Doing so will only create more resistance on his part. Reach down and slide the dog's feet toward you until he is lying down.

An alternative method of getting your Pom into the down position is to move around to the dog's right side and, as you draw his attention downward with your right hand, slide your left hand under the dog's front legs, gently sliding them forward. You will undoubtedly have to be on your knees next to the puppy in order to do this.

As your dog's forelegs begin to slide out in front of him, keep moving the treat along the floor until his entire body is lying on the ground, while continually repeating the word, "Down." Once your dog has assumed the position you desire, give him the treat and a lot of praise. Continue assisting your Pom into the down position until he does it on his own. Be firm and be patient.

The Heel Command

In learning to heel, your Pom will walk on your left side with his shoulder next to your leg, no matter which direction you might go or how quickly you turn. Learning this command can be an extremely valuable lesson for your dog, even though it is a Toy breed. A Pom that darts back and forth in front of or under his master's feet can endanger himself and cause serious injury to his owner, as well.

Teaching your Pom to heel is critical to off-leash control and will not only make your daily walks far more enjoyable, it will make him a more tractable companion when the two of you are in crowded or confusing situations. We do not recommend ever allowing your Pom to be off leash when you are away from home. It is important to know, however, that you can control your dog no matter what the circumstances are.

A lightweight, rounded leather collar or a small jeweler's snake chain is best for training long-

Little Chloe, owned by Christine Jaffe, performs the down command with a smile.

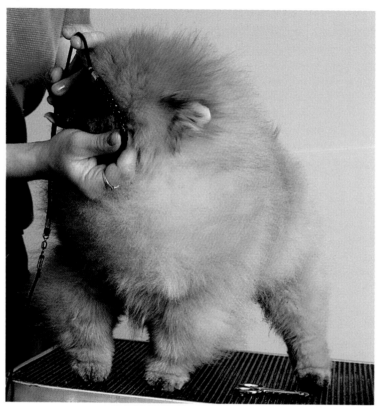

Remember that the attention span of a young dog is like a child's, so keep lessons short, be repetitive, and finish with lots of praise.

haired Toy dogs, especially for the heel lesson. Changing from the collar your dog regularly wears to something different indicates that what you are about to do is "business" and not a casual stroll. The pet shop where you purchase your other supplies can probably assist you in selecting a training collar that will be best for your lessons won't catch in your dog's hair.

As you train your Pom to walk on the leash, you should also teach the puppy to walk on your left side. The leash should cross your body from the dog's collar to your right hand. The excess portion of the leash will be folded into your right hand, and you will use your left hand on the leash to make corrections.

A quick, gentle jerk on the leash with your left hand will keep your dog from lunging side to side, pulling ahead, or darting between your legs. As you make a correction, give the heel command. Keep the leash loose when your dog maintains the proper position at your side. If your dog begins to drift away, give the leash a quick jerk and guide the dog back to the correct position as you give the heel command. Do not pull on the leash with steady pressure. What is needed is a sharp but gentle, jerking motion to get your dog's attention.

TRAINING CLASSES

There are countless things a patient, consistent Pom owner can teach his or her dog. Poms are highly trainable. Remember, the breed has a lifelong history of striving to please. Once lessons are mastered, you will find that most Poms will perform with enthusiasm and gusto, making all the hard work well worthwhile.

Training classes are particularly good because your dog is learning to obey commands despite the distraction of all of the interesting sights and smells of other dogs. There are free-of-charge classes at many parks and recreation facilities, as well as very formal, and sometimes very expensive, individual lessons with private trainers.

Some obedience schools can also train your Pom for you. However, unless your schedule does not provide any time to train your dog, having someone else train him for you would be last on our list of recommendations. The rapport that develops between the owner who has trained his or her Pom and the dog himself is incomparable. The effort you expend to teach your dog to be a pleasant companion and good canine citizen pays off in years of enjoyable companionship.

VERSATILITY

There is no end to the number of activities you and your Pom can enjoy together. The breed is highly successful in both conformation shows and obedience trials in the US.

There are Canine Good Citizen certificates that can be earned through the American Kennel Club and a new event called agility trials. The agility trials are actually "obstacle courses" for dogs and are not only fun for dog and owner, but Pom owners find their little dogs enjoy the exercises as much as they do.

Owners not inclined toward competitive events might find enjoyment in having their Poms serve as therapy dogs. Dogs used in this area are trained to assist the sick, the elderly, and often the handicapped.

Poms have shown themselves to be of outstanding assistance to the hearing impaired. Signaling their owners at the sound of the phone, doorbell, or someone knocking or calling can be a helpful addition to someone's life.

Other therapy dogs make visits to hospitals and homes for the aged. It has been proven that these visits provide great therapeutic value to patients.

Don't let life pass your Pomeranian by! Proper training will allow him to participate in all the excitement that life has to offer.

The well-trained Pom can offer a whole world of activities to his owner. You are limited only by the amount of time you wish to invest in this remarkable breed.

SPORT of Purebred Dogs

Welcome to the exciting and sometimes frustrating sport of dogs. No doubt you are trying to learn more about dogs or you wouldn't be deep into this book. This section covers the basics that may entice you, further your knowledge and help you to understand the dog world.

Dog showing has been a very popular sport for a long time and has been taken quite seriously by some. Others only enjoy it as a hobby.

The Kennel Club in England was formed in 1859, the American Kennel Club was established in 1884 and the Canadian Kennel Club was formed in 1888. The purpose of these clubs was to register purebred dogs and maintain their Stud Books. In the beginning, the concept of registering dogs was not readily accepted. More than 36 million dogs have been enrolled in the AKC Stud Book since its inception in 1888. Presently the kennel clubs not only register dogs but adopt and enforce rules and regulations governing dog shows, obedience trials and field trials. Over the years they have fostered and encouraged interest in the health and welfare of the purebred dog. They routinely donate funds to veterinary research for study on genetic disorders.

The time you invest in training your Pomeranian will benefit the both of you for a lifetime.

Below are the addresses of the kennel clubs in the United States, Great Britain and Canada.

The American Kennel Club
51 Madison Avenue
New York, NY 10010
(Their registry is located at: 5580 Centerview Drive, STE 200, Raleigh, NC 27606-3390)

The Kennel Club
1 Clarges Street
Piccadilly, London, WIY 8AB, England

The Canadian Kennel Club
100-89 Skyway Avenue
Etobicoke, Ontario M6S 4V7
Canada

Today there are numerous activities that are enjoyable for both the dog and the handler. Some of the activities include conformation showing, obedience competition, tracking, agility, the Canine Good Citizen Certificate, and a wide range of instinct tests that vary from breed to breed. Where you start depends upon your goals which early on may not be readily apparent.

PUPPY KINDERGARTEN

Every puppy will benefit from this class. PKT is the foundation for all future dog activities from conformation to "couch potatoes." Pet owners should make an effort to attend even if they never expect to show their dog. The class is designed for puppies about three months of age with graduation at approximately five months of age. All the puppies will be in the same age group and, even though some may be a little unruly, there should not be any real problem. This class will teach the puppy some beginning obedience. As in all obedience classes the owner learns how to train his own dog. The PKT class gives the puppy the opportunity to interact with other puppies in the same age group and exposes him to strangers, which is very important. Some dogs grow up with behavior problems, one of them being fear of strangers. As you can see, there can be much to gain from this class.

There are some basic obedience exercises that every dog should learn. Some of these can be started with puppy kindergarten.

CONFORMATION

Conformation showing is our oldest dog show sport. This type of showing is based on the dog's appearance—that is his structure, movement and attitude. When considering this type of showing, you need to be aware of your breed's standard and be able to evaluate your dog compared to that standard. The breeder of your puppy or other experienced breeders would be good sources for such an evaluation. Puppies can go through lots of changes over a period of time. Many puppies start out as promising hopefuls and then after maturing may be disappointing as show candidates. Even so this should not deter them from being excellent pets.

Usually conformation training classes are offered by the local kennel or obedience clubs. These are excellent places for training puppies. The puppy should be able to walk on a lead before entering such a class. Proper ring procedure and technique for posing (stacking) the dog will be demonstrated as well as gaiting the dog. Usually certain patterns are used in the ring such as the triangle or the "L." Conformation class, like the PKT class, will give your youngster the opportunity to socialize with different breeds of dogs and humans too.

It takes some time to learn the routine of conformation showing. Usually one starts at the puppy matches that may be AKC Sanctioned or Fun Matches. These matches are generally for puppies from two or three months to a year old, and there may be classes for the adult over

With training, who knows how far your Pom can go? The author's Ch. Moreno's Buttercup earned her championship at seven months of age.

the age of 12 months. Similar to point shows, the classes are divided by sex and after completion of the classes in that breed or variety, the class winners compete for Best of Breed or Variety. The winner goes on to compete in the Group and the Group winners compete for Best in Match. No championship points are awarded for match wins.

A few matches can be great training for puppies even though there is no intention to go on showing. Matches enable the puppy to meet new people and be handled by a stranger—the judge. It is also a change of environment, which broadens the horizon for both dog and handler. Matches and other dog activities boost the confidence of the handler and especially the younger handlers.

Earning an AKC championship is built on a point system, which is different from Great Britain. To become an AKC Champion of Record the dog must earn 15 points. The number of points earned each time depends upon the number of dogs in competition. The number of points available at each show depends upon the breed, its sex and the location of the show. The United States is divided into ten AKC zones. Each zone has its own set of points. The purpose of the zones is to try to equalize the points available from breed to breed and area to area.The AKC adjusts the point scale annually.

The number of points that can be won at a show are between one and five. Three-, four- and five-point wins are considered majors. Not only does the dog need 15 points won under three different judges, but those points must include two majors under two different judges. Canada also works on a point system but majors are not required.

Dogs always show before bitches. The classes available to those seeking points are: Puppy (which may be divided into 6 to 9 months and 9 to 12 months); 12 to 18 months; Novice; Bred-by-Exhibitor; American-bred; and Open. The class winners of the same sex of each breed or variety compete against each other for Winners Dog and Winners Bitch. A Reserve Winners Dog and Reserve Winners Bitch are also awarded but do not carry any points unless the Winners win is disallowed by AKC. The Winners Dog and Bitch compete with the specials (those dogs that have attained championship) for Best of Breed or Variety, Best of Winners and Best of Opposite Sex. It is possible to pick up an extra point or even a major if the points are higher for the defeated winner than those of Best of Winners. The latter would get the higher total from the defeated winner.

At an all-breed show, each Best of Breed or Variety winner will go on to his respective Group and then the Group winners will compete against each other for Best in Show. There are seven Groups: Sporting, Hounds, Working, Terriers, Toys, Non-Sporting and Herding. Obviously there are no Groups at speciality shows (those shows that have only one breed or a show such as the American Spaniel Club's Flushing Spaniel Show, which is for all flushing spaniel breeds).

In conformation, your Pomeranian will be judged on how closely he conforms to the standard of the breed.

Earning a championship in England is somewhat different since they do not have a point system. Challenge Certificates are awarded if the judge feels the dog is deserving regardless of the number of dogs in competition. A dog must earn three Challenge Certificates under three different judges, with at least one of these Certificates being won after the age of 12 months. Competition is very strong and entries may be higher than they are in the U.S. The Kennel Club's Challenge Certificates are only available at Championship Shows.

In England, The Kennel Club regulations require that certain dogs, Border Collies and Gundog breeds, qualify in a working capacity (i.e., obedience or field trials) before becoming a full Champion. If they do not qualify in the working aspect, then they are designated a Show Champion, which is equivalent to the AKC's Champion of Record. A Gundog may be granted the title of Field Trial Champion (FT Ch.) if it passes all the tests in the field but would also have to qualify in conformation before becoming a full Champion. A Border Collie that earns the title of Obedience Champion (Ob Ch.) must also qualify in the conformation ring before becoming a Champion.

The U.S. doesn't have a designation full Champion but does award for Dual and Triple Champions. The Dual Champion must be a Champion of Record, and either Champion Tracker, Herding Champion, Obedience Trial Champion or Field Champion. Any dog that has been awarded the titles of Champion of Record, and any two of the following: Champion Tracker, Herding Champion, Obedience Trial Champion or Field Champion, may be designated as a Triple Champion.

The shows in England seem to put more emphasis on breeder judges than those in the U.S. There is much competition within the breeds. Therefore the quality of the individual breeds should be very good. In the United States we tend to have more "all around judges" (those that judge multiple breeds) and use the breeder judges at the specialty shows. Breeder judges are more familiar with their own breed since they

The Westminster Kennel Club is the most prestigious dog show in the United States. Am. Can. Ch. Moreno's Perri Winkle struts his stuff at Westminster.

Successful showing requires dedication and hard work, but most of all, it should be enjoyable for both the dog and his handler.

are actively breeding that breed or did so at one time. Americans emphasize Group and Best in Show wins and promote them accordingly.

The shows in England can be very large and extend over several days, with the Groups being scheduled on different days. Though multi-day shows are not common in the U.S., there are cluster shows, where several different clubs will use the same show site over consecutive days.

Westminster Kennel Club is our most prestigious show although the entry is limited to 2500. In recent years, entry has been limited to Champions. This show is more formal than the majority of the shows with the judges wearing formal attire and the handlers fashionably dressed. In most instances the quality of the dogs is superb. After all, it is a show of Champions. It is a good show to study the AKC registered breeds and is by far the most exciting—especially since it is televised! WKC is one of the few shows in this country that is still benched. This means the dog must be in his benched area during the show hours except when he is being groomed, in the ring, or being exercised.

Typically, the handlers are very particular about their appearances. They are careful not to wear something that will detract from their dog but will perhaps enhance it. American ring procedure is quite formal compared to that of other countries. There is a certain etiquette expected between the judge and exhibitor and among the other exhibitors. Of course it is not always the case but the judge is supposed to be polite, not engaging in small talk or acknowledging how well he knows the handler. There is a more informal and relaxed atmosphere at the shows in other countries. For instance, the dress code is more casual. I can see where this might be more fun for the exhibitor and especially for the novice. The U.S. is very handler-oriented in many of the breeds. It is true, in most instances, that the experienced professional handler can present the dog better and will have a feel for what a judge likes.

A future show-dog-in-training, this four-month-old Pomeranian practices standing at attention and awaits his owner's next command.

In England, Crufts is The Kennel Club's own show and is most assuredly the largest dog show in the world. They've been known to have an entry of nearly 20,000, and the show lasts four days. Entry is only gained by qualifying through winning in specified classes at another Championship Show. Westminster is strictly conformation, but Crufts exhibitors and spectators enjoy not only conformation but obedience, agility and a multitude of exhibitions as well. Obedience was admitted in 1957 and agility in 1983.

If you are handling your own dog, please give some consideration to your apparel. For sure the dress code at matches is more informal than the point shows. However, you should wear something a little more appropriate than beach attire or ragged jeans and bare feet. If you check out the handlers and see what is presently fashionable, you'll catch on. Men usually dress with a shirt and tie and a nice sports coat. Whether you are male or female, you will want to wear comfortable clothes and shoes. You need to be able to run with your dog and

To the victor go the spoils! This pretty Pom proudly shows off her many medals and awards.

you certainly don't want to take a chance of falling and hurting yourself. Heaven forbid, if nothing else, you'll upset your dog. Women usually wear a dress or two-piece outfit, preferably with pockets to carry bait, comb, brush, etc. In this case men are the lucky ones with all their pockets. Ladies, think about where your dress will be if you need to kneel on the floor and also think about running. Does it allow freedom to do so?

You need to take along dog; crate; ex pen (if you use one); extra newspaper; water pail and water; all required grooming equipment, including hair dryer and extension cord; table; chair for you; bait for dog and lunch for you and friends; and, last but not least, clean up materials, such as plastic bags, paper towels, and perhaps a bath towel and some shampoo—

The well-bred Pomeranian makes an outstanding show dog that can be easily handled by children as well as adults.

just in case. Don't forget your entry confirmation and directions to the show.

If you are showing in obedience, then you will want

to wear pants. Many of our top obedience handlers wear pants that are color-coordinated with their dogs. The philosophy is that imperfections in the black dog will be less obvious next to your black pants.

Whether you are showing in conformation, Junior Showmanship or obedience, you need to watch the clock and be sure you are not late. It is customary to pick up your conformation armband a few minutes before the start of the class. They will not wait for you and if you are on the show grounds and not in the ring, you will upset everyone. It's a little more complicated picking up your obedience armband if you show later in the class. If you have not picked up your armband and they get to your number, you may not be allowed to show. It's best to pick up your armband early, but then you may show earlier than expected if other handlers don't pick up. Customarily all conflicts should be discussed with the judge prior to the start of the class.

There are many activities and events in which your Pomeranian can participate, and the versatile breed has the ability to excel at them all.

Junior Showmanship

The Junior Showmanship Class is a wonderful way to build self confidence even if there are no aspirations of staying with the dog-show game later in life. Frequently, Junior Showmanship becomes the background of those who become successful exhibitors/handlers in the future. In some instances it is taken very seriously, and success is measured in terms of wins. The Junior Handler is judged solely on his ability and skill in presenting his dog. The dog's conformation is not to be considered by the judge. Even so the condition and grooming of the dog may be a reflection upon the handler.

Usually the matches and point shows include different classes. The Junior Handler's dog may be entered in a breed or obedience class and even shown by another person in that class.

Junior Showmanship classes are usually divided by age and perhaps sex. The age is determined by the handler's age on the day of the show. The classes are:

CANINE GOOD CITIZEN

The AKC sponsors a program to encourage dog owners to train their dogs. Local clubs perform the pass/fail tests, and dogs who pass are awarded a Canine Good Citizen Certificate. Proof of vaccination is required at the time of participation. The test includes:

1. Accepting a friendly stranger.
2. Sitting politely for petting.
3. Appearance and grooming.
4. Walking on a loose leash.
5. Walking through a crowd.
6. Sit and down on command/staying in place.
7. Come when called.
8. Reaction to another dog.
9. Reactions to distractions.
10. Supervised separation.

If more effort was made by pet owners to accomplish these exercises, fewer dogs would be cast off to the humane shelter.

OBEDIENCE

Obedience is necessary, without a doubt, but it can also become a wonderful hobby or even an obsession. Obedience classes and competition can provide wonderful companionship, not only with your dog but with your classmates or fellow competitors. It is always gratifying to discuss your dog's problems with others who have had similar experiences. The AKC acknowledged Obedience around 1936, and it has changed tremendously even though many of the exercises are basically the same. Today, obedience competition is just that—very competitive. Even so, it is possible for every obedience exhibitor to come home a winner (by earning qualifying scores) even though he/she may not earn a placement in the class.

Most of the obedience titles are awarded after earning three qualifying scores (legs) in the appropriate class under three different judges. These classes offer a perfect score of 200, which is extremely rare. Each of the class exercises has its own point value. A leg is earned after receiving a score of at least 170 and at least 50 percent of the points available in each exercise. The titles are:

Companion Dog
Excellent–CDX
Utility Dog–UD

After achieving the UD title, you may feel inclined to go after the UDX and/or OTCh. The UDX (Utility Dog Excellent) title went into effect in January 1994. It is not easily attained. The title requires qualifying simultaneously ten times in Open B and Utility B but not necessarily at consecutive shows.

The OTCh (Obedience Trial Champion) is awarded after the dog has earned his UD and then goes on to earn 100 championship points, a first place in Utility, a first place in Open and another first place in either class. The placements must be won under three different judges at all-breed obedience trials. The points are determined by the number of dogs competing in the Open B and Utility B classes. The OTCh title precedes the dog's name.

Handlers must pose their Pomeranians in the most flattering position to emphasize the dog's specific strengths.

Obedience matches (AKC Sanctioned, Fun, and Show and Go) are usually available. Usually they are sponsored by the local obedience clubs. When preparing an obedience dog for a title, you will find matches very helpful. Fun Matches and Show and Go Matches are more lenient in allowing you to make corrections in the ring. This type of training is usually very necessary for the Open and Utility Classes. AKC Sanctioned Obedience Matches do not allow corrections in the ring since they must abide by the AKC Obedience Regulations. If you are interested in showing in obedience, then you should contact the AKC for a copy of the Obedience Regulations.

TRACKING

Tracking is officially classified obedience. There are three tracking titles available: Tracking Dog (TD), Tracking Dog Excellent (TDX), Variable Surface Tracking (VST). If all three tracking titles are obtained, then the dog officially becomes a CT (Champion Tracker). The CT will go in front of the dog's name.

A TD may be earned anytime and does not have to follow the other obedience titles. There are many exhibitors that prefer tracking to obedience, and there are others who do both.

AGILITY

Agility was first introduced by John Varley in England at the Crufts Dog Show, February 1978, but Peter Meanwell, competitor and judge, actually developed the idea. It was officially recognized in the early '80s. Agility is extremely popular in England and Canada and growing in popularity in the U.S. The AKC acknowledged agility in August 1994. Dogs must be at least 12 months of age to be entered. It is a fascinating sport that the dog, handler and spectators enjoy to the utmost. Agility is a spectator sport! The dog performs off lead. The handler either runs with his dog or positions himself on the course and directs his dog with verbal and hand signals over a timed course over or through a variety of obstacles including a time out or pause. One of the main drawbacks to agility is finding a place to train. The obstacles take up a lot of

Good grooming is essential to a Pomeranian's success in the show ring.

107

Training your Pomeranian will be easier once he is accustomed to wearing a leash.

space and it is very time consuming to put up and take down courses.

The titles earned at AKC agility trials are Novice Agility Dog (NAD), Open Agility Dog (OAD), Agility Dog Excellent (ADX), and Master Agility Excellent (MAX). In order to acquire an agility title, a dog must earn a qualifying score in its respective class on three separate occasions under two different judges. The MAX will be awarded after earning ten qualifying scores in the Agility Excellent Class.

PERFORMANCE TESTS

During the last decade the American Kennel Club has promoted performance tests–those events that test the different breeds' natural abilities. This type of event encourages a handler to devote even more time to his dog and retain the natural instincts of his breed heritage. It is an important part of the wonderful world of dogs.

Obedience, tracking and agility allow the purebred dog with an Indefinite Listing Privilege (ILP) number or a limited registration to be exhibited and earn titles. Application must be made to the AKC for an ILP number.

The American Kennel Club publishes a monthly *Events* magazine that is part of the *Gazette*, their official journal for the sport of purebred dogs. The *Events* section lists upcoming shows and the secretary or superintendent for them. The majority of the conformation shows in the U.S. are overseen by licensed superintendents. Generally the entry closing date is approximately two-and-a-half weeks before the actual show. Point shows are fairly expensive, while the match shows cost about one third of the point show entry fee. Match shows usually take entries the day of the show but some are pre-entry. The best way to find match show information is through your local kennel club. Upon asking, the AKC can provide you with a list of superintendents, and you can write and ask to be put on their mailing lists.

Even if you never enter your Pomeranian in a dog competition, the time spent in training will strengthen the bond between owner and dog.

Obedience trial and tracking test information is available through the AKC. Frequently these events are not superintended, but put on by the host club. Therefore you would make the entry with the event's secretary.

As you have read, there are numerous activities you can share with your dog. Regardless what you do, it does take teamwork. Your dog can only benefit from your attention and training. We hope this chapter has enlightened you and hope, if nothing else, you will attend a show here and there. Perhaps you will start with a puppy kindergarten class, and who knows where it may lead!

HEALTH CARE

Veterinary medicine has become far more sophisticated than what was available to our ancestors. This can be attributed to the increase in household pets and consequently the demand for better care for them. Also human medicine has become far more complex. Today diagnostic testing in veterinary medicine parallels human diagnostics. Because of better technology we can expect our pets to live healthier lives thereby increasing their life spans.

THE FIRST CHECKUP

You will want to take your new puppy/dog in for its first checkup within 48 to 72 hours after acquiring it. Many breeders strongly recommend this check up and so do the humane shelters. A puppy/dog can appear healthy but it may have a serious problem that is not apparent to the layman. Most pets have some type of a minor flaw that may never cause a real problem.

Unfortunately if he/she should have a serious problem, you will want to consider the consequences of keeping the pet and the attachments that will be formed, which may be broken prematurely. Keep in mind there are many healthy dogs looking for good homes.

This first check up is a good time to establish yourself with the veterinarian and learn the office policy regarding their hours and how they handle emergencies. Usually the breeder or another conscientious pet owner is a good reference for locating a capable veterinarian. You should be aware that not all veterinarians give the same quality of service. Please do not make your selection on the least expensive clinic, as they may be short changing your pet. There is the possibility that eventually it will cost you more due to improper diagnosis, treatment, etc. If you are selecting a new veterinarian, feel free to ask for a tour of the clinic. You should inquire about making an appointment for a tour since all clinics are working clinics, and therefore may not be available all day for sightseers.

You may worry less if you see where your pet will be spending the day if he ever needs to be hospitalized.

THE PHYSICAL EXAM

Your veterinarian will check your pet's overall condition, which includes listening to the heart; checking the respiration; feeling the abdomen, muscles and joints; checking the mouth, which includes the gum color and signs of gum disease along with plaque buildup; checking the ears for signs of an infection or ear mites; examining the eyes; and, last but not least, checking the condition of the skin and coat.

He should ask you questions regarding your pet's eating and elimination habits and invite you to relay your questions. It is a good idea to prepare a list so as not to forget anything. He should discuss the proper diet and the quantity to be fed. If this should differ from your breeder's recommendation, then you should convey to him the breeder's choice and see if he approves. If he recommends changing the diet, then this should be done over a few days so as not to cause a gastrointestinal upset. It is customary to take in a fresh stool sample (just a small amount) for a test for intestinal parasites. It must

Puppies receive immunity from disease while nursing, but after they are weaned they require immunizations to keep them healthy.

111

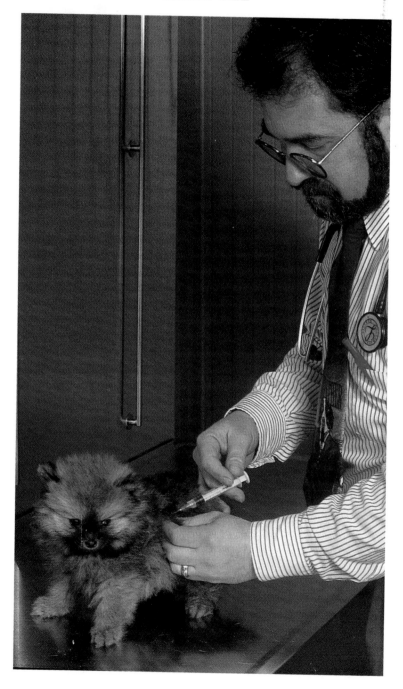

be fresh, preferably within 12 hours, since the eggs hatch quickly and after hatching will not be observed under the microscope. If your pet isn't obliging then, usually the technician can take one in the clinic.

IMMUNIZATIONS

It is important that you take your puppy/dog's vaccination record with you on your first visit. In case of a puppy, presumably the breeder has seen to the vaccinations up to the time you acquired custody. Veterinarians differ in their vaccination protocol. It is not unusual for your puppy to have received vaccinations for distemper, hepatitis, leptospirosis, parvovirus and parainfluenza every two to three weeks from the age of five or six weeks. Usually this is a combined injection and is typically called the DHLPP. The DHLPP is given through at least 12 to 14 weeks of age, and it is customary to continue with another parvovirus vaccine at 16 to 18 weeks. You may wonder why so many immunizations are necessary. No one knows for sure when the puppy's maternal antibodies are gone, although it is customarily accepted that distemper antibodies are gone by 12 weeks. Usually parvovirus antibodies are gone by 16 to 18 weeks of age. However, it is possible for the maternal antibodies to be gone at a much earlier age or even a later age. Therefore immunizations are started at an early age. The vaccine will not give immunity as long as there are maternal antibodies.

The rabies vaccination is given at three or six months of age depending on your local laws. A vaccine for bordetella (kennel cough) is advisable and can be given anytime from the age of five weeks. The coronavirus is not commonly given unless there is a problem locally. The Lyme vaccine is necessary in endemic areas. Lyme disease has been reported in 47 states.

Your veterinarian will set up a vaccination schedule for your Pomeranian. Follow it and continue to get booster shots throughout the dog's lifetime.

Distemper

This is virtually an incurable disease. If the dog recovers, he is subject to severe nervous disorders. The virus attacks every tissue in the body and resembles a bad cold with a fever. It can cause a runny nose and eyes and cause gastrointestinal disorders, including a poor appetite, vomiting and diarrhea. The virus is carried by raccoons, foxes, wolves, mink and other dogs. Unvaccinated youngsters and senior citizens are very susceptible. This is still a common disease.

Hepatitis

This is a virus that is most serious in very young dogs. It is spread by contact with an infected animal or its stool or urine. The virus affects the liver and kidneys and is characterized by high fever, depression and lack of appetite. Recovered animals may be afflicted with chronic illnesses.

Leptospirosis

This is a bacterial disease transmitted by contact with the urine of an infected dog, rat or other wildlife. It produces severe symptoms of fever, depression, jaundice and internal bleeding and was fatal before the vaccine was developed. Recovered dogs can be carriers, and the disease can be transmitted from dogs to humans.

Parvovirus

This was first noted in the late 1970s and is still a fatal disease. However, with proper vaccinations, early diagnosis and prompt treatment, it is a manageable disease. It attacks the bone marrow and intestinal tract. The symptoms include depression, loss of appetite, vomiting, diarrhea and collapse. Immediate medical attention is of the essence.

Bordetella attached to canine cilia. Otherwise known as kennel cough, this disease is highly contagious and should be vaccinated against routinely.

Rabies

This is shed in the saliva and is carried by raccoons, skunks, foxes, other dogs and cats. It attacks nerve tissue, resulting in paralysis and death. Rabies can be transmitted to people and is virtually always fatal. This disease is reappearing in the suburbs.

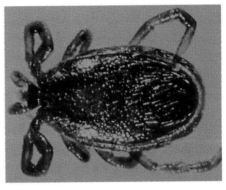

The deer tick is the most common carrier of Lyme disease. Photo courtesy of Virbac Laboratories, Inc., Fort Worth, Texas.

Bordetella (Kennel Cough)

The symptoms are coughing, sneezing, hacking and retching accompanied by nasal discharge usually lasting from a few days to several weeks. There are several disease-producing organisms responsible for this disease. The present vaccines are helpful but do not protect for all the strains. It usually is not life threatening but in some instances it can progress to a serious bronchopneumonia. The disease is highly contagious. The vaccination should be given routinely for dogs that come in contact with other dogs, such as through boarding, training class or visits to the groomer.

Coronavirus

This is usually self limiting and not life threatening. It was first noted in the late '70s about a year before parvovirus. The virus produces a yellow/brown stool and there may be depression, vomiting and diarrhea.

Lyme Disease

This was first diagnosed in the United States in 1976 in Lyme, CT in people who lived in close proximity to the deer tick. Symptoms may include acute lameness, fever, swelling of joints and loss of appetite. Your veterinarian can advise you if you live in an endemic area.

After your puppy has completed his puppy vaccinations, you will continue to booster the DHLPP once a year. It is customary to booster the rabies one year after the first vaccine and then, depending on where you live, it should be boostered every year or every three years. This depends on your local laws. The Lyme and corona vaccines are boostered annually and it is recommended that the bordetella be boostered every six to eight months.

Annual Visit

I would like to impress the importance of the annual check up, which would include the booster vaccinations, check for intestinal parasites and test for heartworm. Today in our very busy world it is rush, rush and see "how much you can get for how little." Unbelievably, some non-veterinary businesses have entered into the vaccination business. More harm than good can come to your dog through improper vaccinations, possibly from inferior vaccines and/or the wrong schedule. More than likely you truly care about your companion dog and over the years you have devoted much time and expense to his well being. Perhaps you are unaware that a vaccination is not just a vaccination. There is more involved. Please, please follow through with regular physical examinations. It is so important for your veterinarian to know your dog and this is especially true during middle age through the geriatric years. More than likely your older dog will require more than one physical a year. The annual physical is good preventive medicine. Through early diagnosis and subsequent treatment your dog can maintain a longer and better quality of life.

Intestinal Parasites

Hookworms

These are almost microscopic intestinal worms that can cause anemia and therefore serious problems, including death, in young puppies. Hookworms can be transmitted to humans through penetration of the skin. Puppies may be born with them.

Roundworms

These are spaghetti-like worms that can cause a potbellied appearance and dull coat along with more severe symptoms, such as vomiting, diarrhea and coughing. Puppies acquire these while in the mother's uterus and through lactation. Both hookworms and roundworms may be acquired through ingestion.

Whipworms

These have a three-month life cycle and are not acquired through the dam. They cause intermittent diarrhea usually with mucus. Whipworms are possibly the most difficult worm to eradicate. Their eggs are very resistant to most environmental factors and can last for years until the proper conditions enable them to mature. Whipworms are seldom seen in the stool.

Intestinal parasites are more prevalent in some areas than others. Climate, soil and contamination are big factors contributing to the incidence of intestinal parasites. Eggs are passed in the stool, lay on the ground and then become infective in a certain number of days. Each of the above worms has a different life cycle. Your best chance of becoming and remaining worm-free is to always pooper-scoop your yard. A fenced-in yard keeps stray dogs out, which is certainly helpful.

Roundworm eggs as seen on a fecal evaluation. The eggs must develop for at least 12 days before becoming infectious.

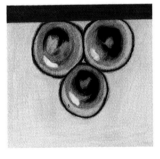

I would recommend having a fecal examination on your dog twice a year or more often if there is a problem. If your dog has a positive fecal sample, then he will be given the appropriate medication and you will be asked to bring back another stool sample in a certain period of time (depending on the type of worm) and then be rewormed. This process goes on until he has at least two negative samples. The different types of worms require different medications. You will be wasting your money and doing your dog an injustice by buying over-the-counter medication without first consulting your veterinarian.

OTHER INTERNAL PARASITES

Coccidiosis and Giardiasis

These protozoal infections usually affect puppies, especially in places where large numbers of puppies are brought together. Older dogs may harbor these infections but do not show signs unless they are stressed. Symptoms include diarrhea, weight loss and lack of appetite. These infections are not always apparent in the fecal examination.

Tapeworms

Seldom apparent on fecal floatation, they are diagnosed frequently as rice-like segments around the dog's anus and the base of the tail. Tapeworms are long, flat and ribbon like, sometimes several feet in length, and made up of many segments about five-eighths of an inch long. The two most common types of tapeworms found in the dog are:

Dirofilaria—adult worms on the heart of a dog. Courtesy of Merck Ag Vet.

(1) First the larval form of the flea tapeworm parasite must mature in an intermediate host, the flea, before it can become infective. Your dog acquires this by ingesting the flea through licking and chewing.

(2) Rabbits, rodents and certain large game animals serve as intermediate hosts for other species of tapeworms. If your dog should eat one of these infected hosts, then he can acquire tapeworms.

HEARTWORM DISEASE

This is a worm that resides in the heart and adjacent blood vessels of the lung that produces microfilaria, which circulate in the bloodstream. It is possible for a dog to be infected with any number of worms from one to a hundred that can be 6 to 14 inches long. It is a life-threatening disease, expensive to treat and easily prevented. Depending on where you live, your veterinarian may recommend a preventive year-round and either an annual or semiannual blood test. The most common preventive is given once a month.

Your Pomeranian can pick up parasites like fleas and ticks after playing outside. Be sure to check your dog's coat thoroughly.

EXTERNAL PARASITES

Fleas

These pests are not only the dog's worst enemy but also enemy to the owner's pocketbook. Preventing is less expensive than treating, but regardless we'd prefer to spend our money elsewhere. Likely, the majority of our dogs are allergic to the bite of a flea, and in many cases it only takes one flea bite. The protein in the flea's saliva is the culprit. Allergic dogs have a reaction, which usually results in a "hot spot." More than likely such a reaction will involve a trip to the veterinarian for treatment. Yes, prevention is less expensive. Fortunately today there are several good products available.

If there is a flea infestation, no one product is going to correct the problem. Not only will the dog require treatment so will the environment. In general flea collars are not very effective although there is now available an "egg" collar that will kill the eggs on the dog. Dips are the most economical but they are messy. There are some effective shampoos and treatments available through pet shops and veterinarians. An oral tablet arrived on the American market in 1995 and was popular in Europe the previous year. It sterilizes the female flea but will not kill adult fleas. Therefore the tablet, which is given monthly, will decrease the flea population but is not a "cure-all." Those dogs that suffer from flea-bite allergy will still be subjected to the bite of the flea. Another popular parasiticide is permethrin, which is applied to the back of the dog in one or two places depending on the dog's weight. This product works as a repellent causing the flea to get "hot feet" and jump off. Do not confuse this product with some of the organophosphates that are also applied to the dog's back.

Some products are not usable on young puppies. Treating fleas should be done under your veterinarian's guidance. Frequently it is necessary to combine

External parasites can cause allergic reactions in your Pomeranian. If your dog is scratching excessively, be sure to check for infestation.

Regular medical care is essential throughout your Pomeranian's adulthood. Annual physical exams are part of his lifelong maintenance.

products and the layman does not have the knowledge regarding possible toxicities. It is hard to believe but there are a few dogs that do have a natural resistance to fleas. Nevertheless it would be wise to treat all pets at the same time. Don't forget your cats. Cats just love to prowl the neighborhood and consequently return with unwanted guests.

Adult fleas live on the dog but their eggs drop off the dog into the environment. There they go through four larval stages before reaching adulthood, and thereby are able to jump back on the poor unsuspecting dog. The cycle resumes and takes between 21 to 28 days under ideal conditions. There are environmental products available that will kill both the adult fleas and the larvae.

Ticks

Ticks carry Rocky Mountain Spotted Fever, Lyme disease and can cause tick paralysis. They should be removed with tweezers, trying to pull out the head. The jaws carry disease. There is a tick preventive collar that does an excellent job. The ticks automatically back out on those dogs wearing collars.

Sarcoptic Mange

This is a mite that is difficult to find on skin scrapings. The pinnal reflex is a good indicator of this disease. Rub the ends of the pinna (ear) together and the dog will start scratching with his foot. Sarcoptes are highly contagious to other dogs and to humans although they do not live long on humans. They cause intense itching.

Responsible breeders will screen all of their Pomeranians for genetic diseases and conditions before breeding them.

Demodectic Mange

This is a mite that is passed from the dam to her puppies. It affects youngsters age three to ten months. Diagnosis is confirmed by skin scraping. Small areas of alopecia around the eyes, lips and/or forelegs become visible. There is little itching unless there is a secondary bacterial infection. Some breeds are afflicted more than others.

Cheyletiella

This causes intense itching and is diagnosed by skin scraping. It lives in the outer layers of the skin of dogs, cats, rabbits and humans. Yellow-gray scales may be found on the back and the rump, top of the head and the nose.

TO BREED OR NOT TO BREED

More than likely your breeder has requested that you have your puppy neutered or spayed. Your breeder's request is based on what is healthiest for your dog and what is most beneficial for your breed. Experienced and conscientious

Spaying or neutering is often the best option for your family pet. It will help to prevent certain diseases of the reproductive system and control the dog population. breeders devote many years into developing a bloodline. In order to do this, he makes every effort to plan each breeding in regard to conformation, temperament and health. This type of breeder does his best to perform the necessary testing (i.e., OFA, CERF, testing for inherited blood disorders, thyroid, etc.).

Testing is expensive and sometimes very disheartening when a favorite dog doesn't pass his health tests. The health history pertains not only to the breeding stock but to the immediate ancestors. Reputable breeders do not want their offspring to be bred indiscriminately. Therefore you may be asked to neuter or spay your puppy. Of course there is always the exception, and your breeder may agree to let you breed your dog under his direct supervision. This is an important concept. More and more effort is being made to breed healthier dogs.

Spay/Neuter

There are numerous benefits of performing this surgery at six months of age. Unspayed females are subject to mammary and ovarian cancer. In order to prevent mammary cancer she must be spayed prior to her first heat cycle. Later in life, an unspayed female may develop a pyometra (an infected uterus), which is definitely life threatening.

Spaying is performed under a general anesthetic and is easy on the young dog. As you might expect it is a little harder on the older dog, but that is no reason to deny her the surgery. The surgery removes the ovaries and uterus. It is important to remove all the ovarian tissue. If some is left behind, she could remain attractive to males. In order to view the ovaries, a reasonably long incision is necessary. An ovariohysterectomy is considered major surgery.

Neutering the male at a young age will inhibit some characteristic male behavior that owners frown upon. Some boys will not hike their legs and mark territory if they are neutered at six months of age. Also neutering at a young age has hormonal benefits, lessening the chance of hormonal aggressiveness.

Surgery involves removing the testicles but leaving the scrotum. If there should be a retained testicle, then he definitely needs to be neutered before the age of two or three years. Retained testicles can develop into cancer. Unneutered males are at risk for testicular cancer, perineal fistulas, perianal tumors and fistulas and prostatic disease.

Intact males and females are prone to housebreaking accidents. Females urinate frequently before, during and after heat cycles, and males tend to mark territory if there is a female in heat. Males may show the same behavior if there is a visiting dog or guests.

Surgery involves a sterile operating procedure equivalent to human surgery. The incision site is shaved, surgically scrubbed and draped. The veterinarian wears a sterile surgical gown, cap, mask and gloves. Anesthesia should be monitored by a registered technician. It is customary for the veterinarian to recommend a pre-anesthetic blood screening, looking for metabolic problems and a ECG rhythm strip to check for normal heart function. Today anesthetics are equal to human anesthetics, which enables your dog to walk out of the clinic the same day as surgery.

Some folks worry about their dog gaining weight after being neutered or spayed. This is usually not the case. It is true that some dogs may be less active so they could develop a problem, but most dogs are just as active as they were before surgery. However, if your dog should begin to gain, then you need to decrease his food and see to it that he gets a little more exercise.

All Poms are cute, but not all are of breeding quality. Breeders will often sell pet-quality Poms on the condition that they are spayed or neutered.

DENTAL CARE for Your Dog's Life

So you've got a new puppy! You also have a new set of puppy teeth in your household. Anyone who has ever raised a puppy is abundantly aware of these new teeth. Your puppy will chew anything it can reach, chase your shoelaces, and play "tear the rag" with any piece of clothing it can find. When puppies are newly born, they have no teeth. At about four weeks of age, puppies of most breeds begin to develop their deciduous or baby teeth. They begin eating semi-solid food, fighting and biting with their litter mates, and learning discipline from their mother. As their new teeth come in, they inflict more pain on their mother's breasts, so her feeding sessions become less frequent and shorter. By six or eight weeks, the mother will start growling to warn her pups when they are fighting too roughly or hurting her as they nurse too much with their new teeth.

A thorough oral exam should be a part of your Pomeranian's regular veterinary checkup.

Puppies need to chew. It is a necessary part of their physical and mental development. They develop

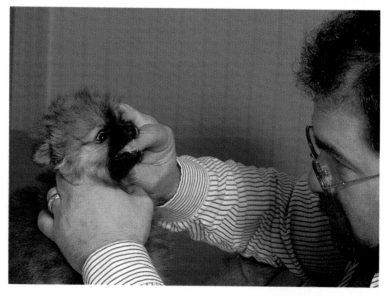

126

Safe toys can alleviate your Pom's need to chew and exercise his mouth and gums.

muscles and necessary life skills as they drag objects around, fight over possession, and vocalize alerts and warnings. Puppies chew on things to explore their world. They are using their sense of taste to determine what is food and what is not. How else can they tell an electrical cord from a lizard? At about four months of age, most puppies begin shedding their baby teeth. Often these teeth need some help to come out and make way for the permanent teeth. The incisors (front teeth) will be replaced first. Then, the adult canine or fang teeth erupt. When the baby tooth is not shed before the permanent tooth comes in, veterinarians call it a retained deciduous tooth. This condition will often cause gum infections by trapping hair and debris between the permanent tooth and the retained baby tooth. Nylafloss® is an excellent device for puppies to use. They can toss it, drag it, and chew on the many surfaces it presents. The baby teeth can catch in the nylon material, aiding in their removal. Puppies that have adequate chew toys will have less destructive behavior, develop more physically, and have less chance of retained deciduous teeth.

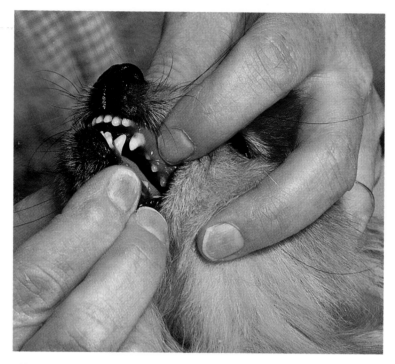

Cleaning your Pom's teeth should be part of your grooming routine.

During the first year, your dog should be seen by your veterinarian at regular intervals. Your veterinarian will let you know when to bring in your puppy for vaccinations and parasite examinations. At each visit, your veterinarian should inspect the lips, teeth, and mouth as part of a complete physical examination. You should take some part in the maintenance of your dog's oral health. You should examine your dog's mouth weekly throughout his first year to make sure there are no sores, foreign objects, tooth problems, etc. If your dog drools excessively, shakes its head, or has bad breath, consult your veterinarian. By the time your dog is six months old, the permanent teeth are all in and plaque can start to accumulate on the tooth surfaces. This is when your dog needs to develop good dental-care habits to prevent calculus build-up on its teeth. Brushing is best. That is a fact that cannot be denied. However, some dogs do not like their teeth brushed regularly, or you may not be able to accomplish the task. In that case, you should consider a product that will help prevent plaque and calculus build-up.

The Plaque Attackers® and Galileo Bone® are other excellent choices for the first three years of a dog's life. Their shapes make them interesting for the dog. As the dog chews on them, the solid polyurethane massages the gums which improves the blood circulation to the periodontal tissues. Projections on the chew devices increase the surface and are in contact with the tooth for more efficient cleaning. The unique shape and consistency prevent your dog from exerting excessive force on his own teeth or from breaking off pieces of the bone. If your dog is an aggressive chewer or weighs more than 55 pounds (25 kg), you should consider giving him a Nylabone®, the most durable chew product on the market.

The Gumabones ®, made by the Nylabone Company, is constructed of strong polyurethane, which is softer than nylon. Less powerful chewers prefer the Gumabones® to the Nylabones®. A super option for your dog is the Hercules Bone®, a uniquely shaped bone named after the great Olympian for its exception strength. Like all Nylabone products, they are specially scented to make them attractive to your dog. Ask your veterinarian about these bones and he will validate the good doctor's prescription: Nylabones® not

The CarrotBone™ by Nylabone® is a healthy and safe chew that your Pomeranian will love.

only give your dog a good chewing workout but also help to save your dog's teeth (and even his life, as it protects him from possible fatal periodontal diseases). By the time dogs are four years old, 75% of them have periodontal disease. It is the most common infection in dogs. Yearly examinations by your veterinarian are essential to maintaining your dog's good health. If your veterinarian detects periodontal disease, he or she may recommend a prophylactic cleaning. To do a thorough cleaning, it will be necessary to put your dog under anesthesia. With modern gas anesthetics and monitoring equipment, the procedure is pretty safe. Your veterinarian will scale the teeth with an ultrasound scaler or hand instrument. This removes the calculus from the teeth. If there are calculus deposits below the gum line, the veterinarian will plane the roots to make them smooth. After all of the calculus has been removed, the teeth are polished with pumice in a polishing cup. If any medical or surgical treatment is needed, it is done at this time. The final step would be fluoride treatment and your follow-up treatment at home. If the periodontal disease is advanced, the veterinarian may prescribe a medicated mouth rinse or antibiotics for use at home. Make sure your dog has safe, clean and attractive chew toys and treats. Chooz® treats are another way of using a consumable treat to help keep your dog's teeth clean.

Rawhide is the most popular of all materials for a dog to chew. This has never been good news to dog owners, because rawhide is inherently very dangerous for dogs. Thousands of dogs have died from rawhide, having swallowed the hide after it has become soft and mushy, only to cause stomach and intestinal blockage. A new rawhide product on the market has finally solved the problem of rawhide: molded Roar-Hide® from Nylabone. These are composed of processed, cut up, and melted American rawhide injected into your dog's favorite shape: a dog bone. These dog-safe devices smell and taste like rawhide but don't break up. The ridges on the bones help to fight tartar build-up on the teeth and they last ten times longer than the usual rawhide chews.

As your dog ages, professional examination and cleaning should become more frequent. The mouth should be inspected at least once a year. Your veterinarian may recommend visits every six months. In the geriatric patient, organs such as the heart, liver, and kidneys do not function as well as when they were young. Your veterinarian will probably want to test these organs' functions prior to using general anesthesia for dental cleaning. If your dog is a good chewer and you work closely with your veterinarian, your dog can keep all of its teeth all of its life. However, as your dog ages, his sense of smell, sight, and taste will diminish. He may not have the desire to chase, trap or chew his toys. He will also not have the energy to chew for long periods, as arthritis and periodontal disease make chewing painful. This will leave you with more responsibility for keeping his teeth clean and healthy. The dog that would not let you brush his teeth at one year of age, may let you brush his teeth now that he is ten years old.

All puppies need to chew, and safe bones and chew toys are important to maintain your Pomeranian's oral health.

If you train your dog with good chewing habits as a puppy, he will have healthier teeth throughout his life.

TRAVELING with Your Dog

The earlier you start traveling with your new puppy or dog, the better. He needs to become accustomed to traveling. However, some dogs are nervous riders and become carsick easily. It is helpful if he starts with an empty stomach. Do not despair, as it will go better if you continue taking him with you on short fun rides. How would you feel if every time you rode in the car you stopped at the doctor's for an injection? You would soon dread that nasty car. Older dogs that tend to get carsick may have more of a problem adjusting to traveling. Those dogs that are having a serious problem may benefit from some medication prescribed by the veterinarian.

Because of his size and accommodating nature, the Pomeranian can accompany you almost anywhere.

Do give your dog a chance to relieve himself before getting into the car. It is a good idea to be prepared for a clean up with a leash, paper towels, bag and terry cloth towel.

The safest place for your dog is in a fiberglass crate, although close confinement can promote carsickness in some dogs. If your dog is nervous you can try letting him ride on the seat next to you or in someone's lap.

An alternative to the crate would be to use a car harness made for dogs and/or a safety strap attached to the harness or collar. Whatever you do, do not let your dog ride in the back of a pickup truck unless he is securely tied on a very short lead. I've seen trucks stop quickly and, even though the dog was tied, it fell out and was dragged.

If you accustom your Pom to car rides when he is young, he will soon be more than happy to go with you.

Another advantage of the crate is that it is a safe place to leave him if you need to run into the store. Otherwise you wouldn't be able to leave the windows down. Keep in mind that while many dogs are overly protective in their crates, this may not be enough to deter dognappers. In some states it is against the law to leave a dog in the car unattended.

Never leave a dog loose in the car wearing a collar and leash. More than one dog has killed himself by hanging. Do not let him put his head out an open window. Foreign debris can be blown into his eyes. When leaving your dog unattended in a car, consider the temperature. It can take less than five

A crate is the safest way for your Pomeranian to travel in a car.

minutes to reach temperatures over 100 degrees Fahrenheit.

TRIPS

Perhaps you are taking a trip. Give consideration to what is best for your dog—traveling with you or boarding. When traveling by car, van or motor home, you need to think ahead about locking your vehicle. In all probability you have many valuables in the car and do not wish to leave it unlocked. Perhaps most valuable and not replaceable is your dog. Give thought to securing your vehicle and providing adequate ventilation for him. Another consideration for you when traveling with your dog is medical problems that may arise and little inconveniences, such as exposure to external parasites. Some areas of the country are quite flea infested. You may want to carry flea spray with you. This is even a good idea when staying in motels. Quite possibly you are not the only occupant of the room.

Unbelievably many motels and even hotels do allow canine guests, even some very first-class ones. Gaines Pet Foods Corporation publishes *Touring With Towser*, a directory of domestic hotels and motels that accommodate guests with dogs. Their address is Gaines TWT, PO Box 5700, Kankakee, IL, 60902. Call ahead to any motel that you may be considering and see if they accept pets. Sometimes it is necessary to pay a deposit against room damage. The management may feel

If you decide to leave your Pomeranian home when you travel, a boarding kennel or pet sitter may be your best option.

reassured if you mention that your dog will be crated. If you do travel with your dog, take along plenty of baggies so that you can clean up after him. When we all do our share in cleaning up, we make it possible for motels to continue accepting our pets. As a matter of fact, you should practice cleaning up everywhere you take your dog.

Depending on where your are traveling, you may need an up-to-date health certificate issued by your veterinarian. It is good policy to take along your dog's medical information, which would include the name, address and phone number of your veterinarian, vaccination record, rabies certificate, and any medication he is taking.

AIR TRAVEL

When traveling by air, you need to contact the airlines to check their policy. Usually you have to make arrangements up to a couple of weeks in advance for traveling with your dog. The airlines require your dog to travel in an airline approved fiberglass crate. Usually these can be purchased through the airlines but they are also readily available in most pet-supply stores. If your dog is not accustomed to a crate, then it is a good idea to get him acclimated to it before your trip. The day of the actual trip you should withhold water about one hour ahead of departure and no food for about 12 hours. The airlines generally have temperature restrictions, which do not allow pets to travel if it is either too cold or too hot. Frequently these restrictions are based on the temperatures at the departure and arrival airports. It's best to inquire about a health certificate. These usually need to be issued within ten days of departure. You should arrange for non-stop, direct flights and if a commuter plane should be involved, check to see if it will carry dogs. Some don't. The Humane Society of the United States has put together a tip sheet for airline traveling. You can receive a copy by sending a self-addressed stamped envelope to:

The Humane Society of the United States
Tip Sheet
2100 L Street NW
Washington, DC 20037.

Regulations differ for traveling outside of the country and are sometimes changed without notice. Well in advance you need to write or call the appropriate consulate or agricultural department for instructions. Some countries have lengthy quarantines (six months), and countries differ in their rabies vaccination requirements. For instance, it may have to be given at least 30 days ahead of your departure.

Do make sure your dog is wearing proper identification including your name, phone number and city. You never know when you might be in an accident and separated from your dog. Or your dog could be frightened and somehow manage to escape and run away.

Another suggestion would be to carry in-case-of-emergency instructions. These would include the address and phone number of a relative or friend, your veterinarian's name, address and phone number, and your dog's medical information.

BOARDING KENNELS

Perhaps you have decided that you need to board your dog. Your veterinarian can recommend a good boarding facility or possibly a pet sitter that will come to your house. It is customary for the boarding kennel to ask for proof of vaccination for the DHLPP, rabies and bordetella vaccine. The bordetella should have been given within six months of boarding. This is for your protection. If they do not ask for this proof I would not board at their kennel. Ask about flea control. Those dogs that suffer flea-bite allergy can get in trouble at a boarding kennel. Unfortunately boarding kennels are limited on how much they are able to do.

For more information on pet sitting, contact NAPPS:
National Association of Professional Pet Sitters
1200 G Street, NW
Suite 760
Washington, DC 20005.

Some pet clinics have technicians that pet sit and technicians that board clinic patients in their homes. This may be an alternative for you. Ask your veterinarian if they have an employee that can help you. There is a definite advantage of having a technician care for your dog, especially if your dog is on medication or is a senior citizen.

The adaptable and fun-loving Pom will welcome a new adventure. Ch. Moreno's C C Jr. relaxes on vacation in Hawaii.

You can write for a copy of *Traveling With Your Pet* from ASPCA, Education Department, 441 E. 92nd Street, New York, NY 10128.

IDENTIFICATION and Finding the Lost Dog

There are several ways of identifying your dog. The old standby is a collar with dog license, rabies, and ID tags. Unfortunately collars have a way of being separated from the dog and tags fall off. We're not suggesting you shouldn't use a collar and tags. If they stay intact and on the dog, they are the quickest way of identification.

For several years owners have been tattooing their dogs. Some tattoos use a number with a registry. Here lies the problem because there are several registries to check. If you wish to tattoo, use your social security number. The humane shelters have the means to

Make sure your Pomeranian wears a leash and collar with tags when you go outside. This will prevent him from becoming separated from you.

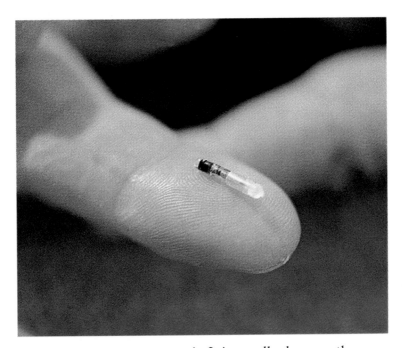

The newest method of identification is the microchip, a chip no bigger than a grain of rice that will help you track your dog's whereabouts.

trace it. It is usually done on the inside of the rear thigh. The area is first shaved and numbed. There is no pain, although a few dogs do not like the buzzing sound. Occasionally tattooing is not legible and needs to be redone.

The newest method of identification is microchipping. The microchip is a computer chip that is no larger than a grain of rice. The veterinarian implants it by injection between the shoulder blades. The dog feels no discomfort. If your dog is lost and picked up by the humane society, they can trace you by scanning the microchip, which has its own code. Microchip scanners are friendly to other brands of microchips and their registries. The microchip comes with a dog tag saying the dog is microchipped. It is the safest way of identifying your dog.

FINDING THE LOST DOG

I am sure you will agree that there would be little worse

than losing your dog. Responsible pet owners rarely lose their dogs. They do not let their dogs run free because they don't want harm to come to them. Not only that but in most, if not all, states there is a leash law.

Beware of fenced-in yards. They can be a hazard. Dogs find ways to escape either over or under the fence. Another fast exit is through the gate that perhaps the neighbor's child left unlocked.

Below is a list that hopefully will be of help to you if you need it. Remember don't give up, keep looking. Your dog is worth your efforts.

1. Contact your neighbors and put flyers with a photo on it in their mailboxes. Information you should include would be the dog's name, breed, sex, color, age, source of identification, when your dog was last seen and where, and your name and phone numbers. It may be helpful to say the dog needs medical care. Offer a *reward*.

2. Check all local shelters daily. It is also possible for your dog to be picked up away from home and end up in an out-of-the-way shelter. Check these too. Go in person. It is not good enough to call. Most shelters are limited on the time they can hold dogs then they are put up for adoption or euthanized. There is the possibility that your dog will not make it to the shelter for several days. Your dog could have been wandering or someone may have tried to keep him.

3. Notify all local veterinarians. Call and send flyers.

4. Call your breeder. Frequently breeders are contacted when one of their breed is found.

5. Contact the rescue group for your breed.

6. Contact local schools—children may have seen your dog.

7. Post flyers at the schools, groceries, gas stations, convenience stores, veterinary clinics, groomers and any other place that will allow them.

Provide your Pomeranian with a safe, enclosed place to play in when he is outside.

8. Advertise in the newspaper.

9. Advertise on the radio.

BEHAVIOR and Canine Communication

S tudies of the human/animal bond point out the importance of the unique relationships that exist between people and their pets. Those of us who share our lives with pets understand the special part they play through companionship, service and protection. For many, the pet/owner bond goes beyond simple companionship; pets are often considered members of the family. A leading pet food manufacturer recently conducted a nationwide survey of pet owners to gauge just how important pets were in their lives. Here's what they found:

Most people consider their Pomeranian to be a valued and important part of the family and thrive on the companionship that a dog provides.

• 76 percent allow their pets to sleep on their beds
• 78 percent think of their pets as their children
• 84 percent display photos of their pets, mostly in their homes
• 84 percent think that their pets react to their own emotions

Dog ownership has been proven to reduce stress and improve the quality of your life. Who could help but smile at these cute Pomeranians?

- 100 percent talk to their pets
- 97 percent think that their pets understand what they're saying

Are you surprised?

Senior citizens show more concern for their own eating habits when they have the responsibility of feeding a dog. Seeing that their dog is routinely exercised encourages the owner to think of schedules that otherwise may seem unimportant to the senior citizen. The older owner may be arthritic and feeling poorly but with responsibility for his dog he has a reason to get up and get moving. It is a big plus if his dog is an attention seeker who will demand such from his owner.

Over the last couple of decades, it has been shown that pets relieve the stress of those who lead busy lives. Owning a pet has been known to lessen the occurrence of heart attack and stroke.

Many single folks thrive on the companionship of a dog. Lifestyles are very different from a long time ago, and today more individuals seek the single life. However, they receive fulfillment from owning a dog.

Most likely the majority of our dogs live in family environments. The companionship they provide is well worth the effort involved. In my opinion, every child should have the opportunity to have a family dog. Dogs teach responsibility through understanding their care, feelings and even respecting their life cycles. Frequently those children who have not been exposed to dogs grow up afraid of dogs, which isn't good. Dogs sense timidity and some will take advantage of the situation.

Children and Pomeranians make great playmates, and caring for a dog can teach a child responsibility and respect for animals.

Today more dogs are serving as service dogs. Since the origination of the Seeing Eye dogs years ago, we now have trained hearing dogs. Also dogs are trained to provide service for the handicapped and are able to perform many different tasks for their owners. Search and Rescue dogs, with their handlers, are sent throughout the world to assist in recovery of disaster victims. They are life savers.

Therapy dogs are very popular with nursing homes, and some hospitals even allow them to visit. The inhabitants truly look forward to their visits. They wanted and were allowed to have visiting dogs in their beds to hold and love.

Nationally there is a Pet Awareness Week to educate students and others about the value and basic care of our pets. Many countries take an even greater interest in their pets than Americans do. In those countries the pets are allowed to accompany their owners into restaurants and shops, etc. In the U.S. this freedom is only available to our service dogs. Even so we think very highly of the human/animal bond.

CANINE BEHAVIOR

Canine behavior problems are the number-one reason for pet owners to dispose of their dogs, either through new homes, humane shelters or euthanasia. Unfortunately there are too many owners who are unwilling to devote the necessary time to properly train their dogs. On the other hand, there are those who not only are concerned about inherited health problems but are also aware of the dog's mental stability.

You may realize that a breed and his group relatives (i.e., sporting, hounds, etc.) show tendencies to behavioral characteristics. An experienced breeder can acquaint you with his breed's personality. Unfortunately many breeds are labeled with poor temperaments when actually the breed as a whole is not affected but only a small percentage of individuals within the breed.

Inheritance and environment contribute to the dog's behavior. Some naïve people suggest inbreeding as the cause of bad temperaments. Inbreeding only results in poor behavior if the ancestors carry the trait. If there are excellent temperaments behind the dogs, then inbreeding will promote good temperaments in the offspring. Did you ever consider that inbreeding is what sets the characteristics of a breed? A purebred dog is the end result of inbreeding. This does not spare the mixed-breed dog from the same problems. Mixed-breed dogs frequently are the offspring of purebred dogs.

Socialization with his dam and littermates will help your Pomeranian get along with other dogs when he is older.

Poms need exercise and stimulation in order to channel their energy into positive pursuits.

Not too many decades ago most of our dogs led a different lifestyle than what is prevalent today. Usually mom stayed home so the dog had human companionship and someone to discipline it if needed. Not much was expected from the dog. Today's mom works and everyone's life is at a much faster pace.

The dog may have to adjust to being a "weekend" dog. The family is gone all day during the week, and the dog is left to his own devices for entertainment. Some dogs sleep all day waiting for their family to come home and others become wigwam wreckers if given the opportunity. Crates do ensure the safety of the dog and the house. However, he could become a physically and emotionally cripple if he doesn't get enough exercise and attention. We still appreciate and want the companionship of our dogs although we expect more from them. In many cases we tend to forget dogs are just that—*dogs* not human beings.

SOCIALIZING AND TRAINING

Many prospective puppy buyers lack experience regarding the proper socialization and training needed to develop the type of pet we all desire. In the first 18 months, training does take some work. It is easier to start proper training before

Children that are raised with dogs usually have a special understanding and bond with them. These three babies look like they get along just fine.

there is a problem that needs to be corrected.

The initial work begins with the breeder. The breeder should start socializing the puppy at five to six weeks of age and cannot let up. Human socializing is critical up through 12 weeks of age and likewise important during the following months. The litter should be left together during the first few weeks but it is necessary to separate them by ten weeks of age. Leaving them together after that time will increase competition for litter dominance. If puppies are not socialized with people by 12 weeks of age, they will be timid in later life.

The eight- to ten-week age period is a fearful time for puppies. They need to be handled very gently around children and adults. There should be no harsh discipline during this time. Starting at 14 weeks of age, the puppy begins the juvenile period, which ends when he reaches sexual maturity around six to 14 months of age. During the juvenile period he needs to be introduced to strangers (adults, children and other dogs) on the home property. At sexual maturity he will begin to bark at strangers and become more protective. Males start to lift their legs to urinate but if you desire you can inhibit this behavior by walking your boy on leash away from trees, shrubs, fences, etc.

Watching a puppy play with his littermate will tell you a lot about his personality. Rusty and Ricco fight for the title of top dog.

Perhaps you are thinking about an older puppy. You need to inquire about the puppy's social experience. If he has lived in a kennel, he may have a hard time adjusting to people and environmental stimuli. Assuming he has had a good social upbringing, there are advantages to an older puppy.

Training includes puppy kindergarten and a minimum of one to two basic training classes. During these classes you will learn how to dominate your youngster. This is especially important if you own a large breed of dog. It is somewhat harder, if not nearly impossible, for some owners to be the Alpha figure when their dog towers over them. You will be taught how to properly restrain your dog. This concept is important. Again it puts you in the Alpha position. All dogs need to be restrained many times during their lives. Believe it or not, some of our worst offenders are the eight-week-old puppies that are brought to our clinic.

They need to be gently restrained for a nail trim but the way they carry on you would think we were killing them. In comparison, their vaccination is a "piece of cake." When we ask dogs to do something that is not agreeable to them, then their worst comes out. Life will be easier for your dog if you expose him at a young age to the necessities of life—proper behavior and restraint.

UNDERSTANDING THE DOG'S LANGUAGE

Most authorities agree that the dog is a descendent of the wolf. The dog and wolf have similar traits. For instance both are pack oriented and prefer not to be isolated for long periods of time. Another characteristic is that the dog, like the wolf, looks to the leader—Alpha—for direction. Both the wolf and the dog communicate through body language, not only within their pack but with outsiders.

A dog's body language can tell you a lot about what she's thinking. Eight-week-old Rosebud tries to show this other "dog" who is the boss.

Every pack has an Alpha figure. The dog looks to you, or should look to you, to be that leader. If your dog doesn't receive the proper training and guidance, he very well may replace you as Alpha. This would be a serious problem and is certainly a disservice to your dog.

Eye contact is one way the Alpha wolf keeps order within his pack. You are Alpha so you must establish eye contact with your puppy. Obviously your puppy will have to look at you. Practice eye contact even if you need to hold his head for five to ten seconds at a time. You can give him a treat as a reward. Make sure your eye contact is gentle and not threatening. Later, if he has been naughty, it is permissible to give him a long, penetrating look. There are some older dogs that never learned eye contact as puppies and cannot accept eye

Every experience that a puppy has will help shape his temperament. Proper socialization from a very young age will help your Pom to get along with anyone.

contact. You should avoid eye contact with these dogs since they feel threatened and will retaliate as such.

BODY LANGUAGE

The play bow, when the forequarters are down and the hindquarters are elevated, is an invitation to play. Puppies play fight, which helps them learn the acceptable limits of biting. This is necessary for later in their lives. Nevertheless, an owner may be falsely reassured by the playful nature of his dog's aggression.

Playful aggression toward another dog or human may be an indication of serious aggression in the future. Owners should never play fight or play tug-of-war with any dog that is inclined to be dominant.

Signs of submission are:
1. Avoids eye contact.
2. Active submission—the dog crouches down, ears back and the tail is lowered.
3. Passive submission—the dog rolls on his side with his hindlegs in the air and frequently urinates.

Signs of dominance are:
1. Makes eye contact.
2. Stands with ears up, tail up and the hair raised on his neck.
3. Shows dominance over another dog by standing at right angles over it.

Dominant dogs tend to behave in characteristic ways such as:
1. The dog may be unwilling to move from his place (i.e., reluctant to give up the sofa if the owner wants to sit there).
2. He may not part with toys or objects in his mouth and may show possessiveness with his food bowl.
3. He may not respond quickly to commands.
4. He may be disagreeable for grooming and dislikes to be petted.

Dogs are popular because of their sociable nature. Those that have contact with humans during the first 12 weeks of life regard them as a member of their own species—their pack. All dogs have the potential for both dominant and submissive behavior. Only through experience and training do they learn to whom it is appropriate to show which behavior. Not all dogs are concerned with dominance but owners need to be aware of that potential. It is wise for the owner to establish his dominance early on.

Your Pomeranian may try to challenge your authority, but he must always know that you are in charge of the relationship.

A human can express dominance or submission toward a dog in the following ways:
1. Meeting the dog's gaze signals dominance. Averting the gaze signals submission. If the dog growls or threatens, averting the

gaze is the first avoiding action to take—it may prevent attack. It is important to establish eye contact in the puppy. The older dog that has not been exposed to eye contact may see it as a threat and will not be willing to submit.

2. Being taller than the dog signals dominance; being lower signals submission. This is why, when attempting to make friends with a strange dog or catch the runaway, one should kneel down to his level. Some owners see their dogs become dominant when allowed on the furniture or on the bed. Then he is at the owner's level.

3. An owner can gain dominance by ignoring all the dog's social initiatives. The owner pays attention to the dog only when he obeys a command.

A reluctance to give up his toys may signal dominant behavior in your Pomeranian. Make sure you offer him the discipline and guidance he needs to succeed in all his endeavors.

No dog should be allowed to achieve dominant status over any adult or child. Ways of preventing are as follows:

1. Handle the puppy gently, especially during the three- to four-month period.

2. Let the children and adults

Your Pomeranian may display fear of new things or situations. Respect his feelings and allow him time to become used to the situation.

handfeed him and teach him to take food without lunging or grabbing.

3. Do not allow him to chase children or joggers.

4. Do not allow him to jump on people or mount their legs. Even females may be inclined to mount. It is not only a male habit.

5. Do not allow him to growl for any reason.

6. Don't participate in wrestling or tug-of-war games.

7. Don't physically punish puppies for aggressive behavior. Restrain him from repeating the infraction and teach an alternative behavior. Dogs should earn everything they receive from their owners. This would include sitting to receive petting or treats, sitting before going out the door and sitting to receive the collar and leash. These types of exercises reinforce the owner's dominance.

Young children should never be left alone with a dog. It is important that children learn some basic obedience commands so they have some control over the dog. They will gain the respect of their dog.

FEAR

One of the most common problems dogs experience is being fearful. Some dogs are more afraid than others. On the lesser side, which is sometimes humorous to watch, dogs can be afraid of a strange object. They act silly when something is out of place in the house. We call his problem perceptive intelligence. He realizes the abnormal within his known environment. He does not react the same way in strange environments since he does not know what is normal.

On the more serious side is a fear of people. This can result in backing off, seeking his own space and saying "leave me alone" or it can result in an aggressive behavior that may lead to challenging the person. Respect that the dog wants to be left alone and give him time to come forward. If you approach the cornered dog, he may resort to snapping. If you leave him alone, he may decide to come forward, which should be rewarded with a treat.

With the proper training and socialization, your Pomeranian will be welcomed anywhere.

Some dogs may initially be too fearful to take treats. In these cases it is helpful to make sure the dog hasn't eaten for about 24 hours. Being a little hungry encourages him to accept the treats, especially if they are of the "gourmet" variety.

Dogs can be afraid of numerous things, including loud noises and thunderstorms. Invariably the owner rewards (by comforting) the dog when it shows signs of fearfulness. When your dog is frightened, direct his attention to something else and act happy. Don't dwell on his fright.

AGGRESSION

Some different types of aggression are: predatory, defensive, dominance, possessive, protective, fear induced, noise provoked, "rage" syndrome (unprovoked aggression), maternal and aggression directed toward other dogs. Aggression is the most common behavioral problem encountered. Protective breeds are expected to be more aggressive than others but with the proper upbringing they can make very dependable companions. You need to be able to read your dog.

Many factors contribute to aggression including genetics and environment. An improper environment, which may include the

living conditions, lack of social life, excessive punishment, being attacked or frightened by an aggressive dog, etc., can all influence a dog's behavior. Even spoiling him and giving too much praise may be detrimental. Isolation and the lack of human contact or exposure to frequent teasing by children or adults also can ruin a good dog.

Lack of direction, fear, or confusion lead to aggression in those dogs that are so inclined. Any obedience exercise, even the sit and down, can direct the dog and overcome fear and/or confusion. Every dog should learn these commands as a youngster, and there should be periodic reinforcement.

When a dog is showing signs of aggression, you should speak calmly (no screaming or hysterics) and firmly give a command that he understands, such as the sit. As soon as your dog obeys, you have assumed your dominant position. Aggression presents a problem because there may be danger to others. Sometimes it is an emotional issue. Owners may consciously or unconsciously encourage their dog's aggression. Other owners show responsibility by accepting the problem and taking measures to keep it under control. The owner is responsible for his dog's actions, and it is not wise to take a chance on someone being bitten, especially a child. Euthanasia is the solution for some owners and in severe cases this may be the best choice. However, few dogs are that dangerous and very few are that much of a threat to their owners. If caution is exercised and professional help is gained early on, most cases can be controlled.

Some authorities recommend feeding a lower protein (less than 20 percent) diet. They believe this can aid in reducing aggression. If the dog loses weight, then vegetable oil can be added. Veterinarians and behaviorists are having some success with pharmacology. In many cases treatment is possible and can improve the situation.

If you have done everything according to "the book" regarding training and socializing and are still having a behavior problem, don't procrastinate. It is important that the problem gets attention before it is out of hand. It is estimated that 20 percent of a veterinarian's time may be devoted to dealing with problems before they become so intolerable that the dog is separated from its home and owner. If your veterinarian isn't able to help, he should refer you to a behaviorist.

SUGGESTED READING

RE-324
*The Guide to Owning
a Pomeranian
64 pages, over 50 full-
color photos*

TS-249
*Owner's Guide to Dog
Health
224 pages, over 190
full-color photos*

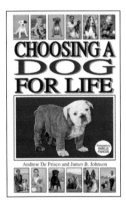

TS-257
*Choosing a Dog for
Life
384 pages, over 700
full-color photos*

JG-117
*A New Owner's Guide to
Dog Training
160 pages, over 140 full-
color photos*

INDEX